1

Give Place
in Your Heart

31 Promises from
the Book of Mormon

Bill Wylson

Other Books by Bill Wylson

Hieroglyphs, Golden Plates and Typos

Seven Success Strategies for Latter-day Saints

Three Minutes Eighteen Seconds

DISCLAIMER

Author's Note: The principles discussed in this work relate to doctrines, procedures and practices of The Church of Jesus Christ of Latter-day Saints. I have attempted to cite sources from the scriptures and from the published writings of the General Authorities of the Church. Nevertheless, I have no authority or commission to speak in any official capacity for the Church. The ideas expressed herein represent nothing more than the opinion of the author.

First Edition published November 2018

ISBN-13:978-0-9904973-6-3

White Horse LDS Books
Salt Lake City, Utah

Edited by Stephen R. Gorton
Artistic Design by Connie Gorton

www.myldsbooks.com

"Now, if ye give place, that a seed may be planted in your heart, behold, if it be a true seed, or a good seed, if ye do not cast it out by your unbelief, that ye will resist the Spirit of the Lord, behold, it will begin to swell within your breasts; and when you feel these swelling motions, ye will begin to say within yourselves – It must needs be that this is a good seed, or that the word is good, for it beginneth to enlarge my soul; yea, it beginneth to enlighten my understanding, yea, it beginneth to be delicious to me."

Alma 32:28

Table of Contents

Chapter One

The Most Correct Book

In the bookcase in the hallway outside of my office rests a copy of the Book of Mormon that belonged to my father before he succumbed to cancer in 2008. It was given to him as a Christmas present in 1942, the year before he went on his first full-time mission.

The leather cover is torn and frayed at the edges. The spine had broken off, been re-attached, and then broke off again. The pages are flavescent with age, worn and dog-eared. Countless verses have been underlined in red pencil and hundreds of notes inscribed in the narrow margins. During his lifetime, my father had read the Book of Mormon, studied it, prayed and pondered for endless hours over it, and had taught incessantly from it.

My wife, in her gentle, delicate voice, told me, "I tried to get him a new set of scriptures once."

"He wouldn't let you, would he?" I replied.

"No," she whispered. "He said when he saw his Savior face-to-face, he wanted to be holding a well-worn set of scriptures.

"He always reminded me of the old saying, 'A Bible that is coming apart at the seams usually indicates that its owner isn't.'"

On the inside cover of this precious book my father had penned in his barely legible handwriting the statement from Joseph Smith, Jr. that reads: *"I told the brethren that the Book of Mormon was the most correct of any book on Earth, and the keystone of our religion, and a man would get nearer to God by abiding by its precepts than by any other book."* [1]

Funk and Wagnall's dictionary defines a keystone as *"the uppermost and last set stone of an arch which completes it and locks its members*

---

[1] Smith, Joseph, *History of The Church of Jesus Christ of Latter-day Saints,* vol. 4, p.461.

together." [2] Another meaning is *"the fundamental element, as of science or doctrine."* [3]

The Book of Mormon, this most correct book, unites and authenticates everlasting principles and eternal edicts encompassing the fundamental doctrines of salvation, making it the keystone of our religion and the gemstone of all our holy scriptures. Moroni's promise that God will manifest the truth of the Book of Mormon to every faithful and sincere inquirer guarantees every individual's right to receive a testimony of the divinity of the Book of Mormon. [4]

"If it is true, this whole system of religion is true because God's hand is in it; if it is not true, then our system of religion is false. But thanks be to God, this book is true! And thanks be to him also, he is willing, desirous, by the power of his Spirit, to bear record of that fact to all honest truth seekers....

"...I quote the words that God himself said in bearing record of the divinity of the Book of Mormon, and make them my testimony also. He said of Joseph

---

[2] Funk and Wagnalls *New Practical Standard Dictionary, Britannica World Language* Edition, 2 vols., 1956, 1:735.
[3] Ibid.
[4] Moroni 10:4.

Smith, 'he has translated the book, even that part which I have commanded him, and as your Lord and your God liveth it is true.'" [5] [6]

Jeffery R. Holland refers to this critical keystone topic as a *"sudden death"* proposition. In his book, *Christ and the New Covenant: The Messianic Message of the Book of Mormon*, Elder Holland writes the following:

"The Prophet Joseph's expression that the Book of Mormon is 'the keystone of our religion' is a profound and crucial observation. A keystone is positioned at the uppermost center of an arch in such a way as to hold all the other stones in place. That key piece, if removed, will bring all of the other blocks crashing down with it. The truthfulness of the Book of Mormon—its origins, its doctrines, and the circumstances of its coming forth—is central to the truthfulness of The Church of Jesus Christ of Latter-day Saints.

"To consider that everything of saving significance in the Church stands or falls on the truthfulness of the Book of Mormon and, by implication, the Prophet Joseph Smith's account of

---

[5] D&C 17:6.
[6] McConkie, Bruce R., *Conference Report*, April 1965.

how it came forth is as sobering as it is true. It is a 'sudden death' proposition. Either the Book of Mormon is what the Prophet Joseph said it is, or this church and its founder are false, a deception from the first instance onward.

"Not everything in life is so black and white, but the authenticity of the Book of Mormon and its keystone role in our religion seem to be exactly that." [7]

I received my first leather-bound copy of the Book of Mormon from my father on my seventeenth birthday. I began carrying the book in my jacket pocket everywhere I went. I studied it intently, marking every verse that impressed me as significant to my life and my personal eternal progress. But my profound testimony of the Book of Mormon did not come to me as an unearned legacy.

I believe that a true understanding and testimony of this critical work comes only with singleness of mind and a strong purpose of heart. When Moroni counseled us to *"ask God, the Eternal Father, in the name of Christ, if these things are not true,"* he also made it clear that we must ask:

---

[7] Holland, Jeffery R., *Christ and the New Covenant: The Messianic Message of the Book of Mormon*, Deseret Book Company, 1997.

1. *"with a sincere heart,*

2. *with real intent,*

3. *having faith in Christ."*

Then will God *"manifest the truth of it unto you, by the power of the Holy Ghost."* [8]

Two years after I was given my own copy of the Book of Mormon, while serving as a full-time missionary, I still had not received that burning manifestation promised by Moroni. I believed with all my heart in the truthfulness of the Book of Mormon, yet I was concerned that my belief would not be a strong enough witness in the face of possible opposition. I went off alone one evening to pray. I always felt I prayed with a sincere heart but that night I prayed with faith and all the real intent I could muster.

I spent three full hours on my knees in prayer and the attendant effort was well worth the results. Moroni's promise was verified as the power of the Holy Ghost filled my heart and witnessed to me that the Book of Mormon is the word of God.

With that confirming testimony of the Book of Mormon came a genuine assurance that Jesus is the

---

[8] Moroni 10:4.

Christ, the Eternal God, as well as the spiritual verification of the divine calling of Joseph Smith. From these basic truths flowed an awareness and comprehension of the other saving principles of the fullness of the gospel and a confirmation of the restoration of the gospel of Jesus Christ, including the divine mission of The Church of Jesus Christ of Latter-day Saints.

As the most correct book on earth, the Book of Mormon was *"written by way of commandment, and also by the spirit of prophecy and of revelation... to the convincing of the Jew and Gentile that Jesus is the Christ, the Eternal God, manifesting himself unto all nations."* [9] It is a substantiating verification of the birth, life, crucifixion and resurrection of Jesus. It is yet another witness of his work as the Messiah and the Redeemer.

Nephi challenges all the ends of the earth to *"harken unto these words and believe in Christ; and if ye believe not in these words believe in Christ. And if ye shall believe in Christ ye will believe in these words, for they are the words of Christ."* [10]

---

[9] Title Page, *The Book of Mormon.*
[10] 2 Nephi 33:10.

A testimony of the truthfulness of the Book of Mormon is founded on spiritual power. The primary assertion of the Book of Mormon, that Jesus is the Christ, the divine Son of God, is spiritual in nature. Things of the Spirit are known only through the power of the Spirit. You cannot gain a witness of a spiritual truth through physical evidence alone. The test for understanding this most correct and sacred book is preeminently spiritual. Seeking a testimony with secular skills rather than with spiritual perception will reveal little of its meaning and message.

Heavenly Father may provide us with additional witnesses and proof that the statements of the Book of Mormon are true, but such proof comes only *after* the exercise of faith. As Moroni stated: *"I... would show unto the world that faith is things which are hoped for and not seen; wherefore, dispute not because ye see not, for ye receive no witness until after the trial of your faith."* [11]

The pronounced importance of the Book of Mormon was affirmed by the Savior himself. He declared: *"This is my doctrine, and it is the doctrine which the Father hath given unto me."* [12]

---

[11] Ether 12:6.

[12] 3 Nephi 11:32.

Jesus is the Christ and the Book of Mormon and Old Testament prophecies concerning his coming have been fulfilled. I testify with the indisputable certainty from the witness of the Holy Spirit that the Book of Mormon is the most correct of any book on earth and that it is possible for everyone to recognize its truthfulness with absolute confidence and conviction. We can obtain a more complete and certain knowledge than intellectual learning alone can ever provide. God himself has revealed: "*As your Lord and your God liveth it is true.*" [13]

Ralph Waldo Emerson is purported to have said: "*I can no more remember the books that I have read than the meals that I have eaten, but they have made me.*"

Today, alongside the old, tattered leather-bound copy of my father's first Book of Mormon, sits my own leather-bound copy of the Book of Mormon. And while these days most of my scripture study is done on electronic devices, I can see how my father treasured his worn-out Book of Mormon. The keystone of our religion and the most correct of any book on earth is firmly in place, shouldering the credence of truth to all the world.

---

[13] D&C 17:6.

The Book of Mormon is true, and it is of the Lord. Its proclamation to the world is that God lives, and Jesus is the Christ. Nothing will serve better at building our faith and testimonies and touching the hearts of honest seekers after truth than this valuable and influential book.

"In saying that the Book of Mormon was the most correct of any book on earth," writes Robert Millet and Joseph Fielding McConkie, *"the Prophet had reference to the doctrines and principles which it taught. The greatest miracle associated with the Book of Mormon is the purity of its doctrines. The true test of its authenticity is found in living those doctrines. The Prophet's promise was that those doing so will get nearer to God than they could by following the precepts of any other book. So it is that the Book of Mormon invites investigation—it extends to all who are honest in heart the invitation to ask God if it is true, with the promise that an answer will be forthcoming."* [14]

One of the most powerful reasons for reading, studying and pondering the principles and doctrines of the Book of Mormon is that it will draw us nearer to God. Anyone harboring a deep longing in their hearts to feel closer to God, to become progressively more like

---

[14] Millet, Robert L. & McConkie, Joseph Fielding, *Joseph Smith: The Choice Seer*, Deseret Book Company.

him in their daily lives, to feel his presence continually will find greater help through the Book of Mormon than through any other book.

Everyone who prayerfully studies the Book of Mormon can gain a testimony of its divinity. Read the Book of Mormon. It will bring you closer to the Lord and his loving power. Christ has promised that those who live by the precepts of this book *"shall receive a crown of eternal life."* [15]

---

[15] D&C 20:14

Chapter Two

The Keystone of Our Lives

The Prophet Joseph Smith affirmed that *"the Book of Mormon [is] ...the keystone of our religion."* [16] It is that crucial, all-important stone in the arch that upholds and supports all the other stones in their respective positions. And if removed, the entire arch would then collapse.

President Marion G. Romney has stated: *"Whatever else it implies, this statement is amply justified by the fact that acceptance of the Book of Mormon is almost tantamount to acceptance of the restored gospel. The authenticity of the book and the restoration of the gospel rest upon the same two*

---

[16] Smith, Joseph, *History of The Church of Jesus Christ of Latter-day Saints,* vol. 4, p.461.

fundamentals—the fact of modern revelation and the fact that Joseph Smith was a prophet of God. These two verities are inseparably connected in their relationship to the Book of Mormon and the restored gospel. To accept one is to accept the other." [17]

So, what is it about the Book of Mormon that makes it the fundamental keystone in our religion? In his book, *A Witness and a Warning,* Ezra Taft Benson highlights a few of the ways the Book of Mormon serves as the keystone of our religion. Along with President Benson's insights, I have included below some of the thoughts and perceptions of other authoritative writers on this subject.

Above all, the Book of Mormon is the keystone of our witness to the world that Jesus is the Christ, the Son of the Eternal Father.

- **The Keystone in Our Witness of Christ.**

The principal purpose of the Book of Mormon stated on the title page is *"to the convincing of the Jew and Gentile that Jesus is the Christ, the Eternal God."* [18] It is undeniably Jesus Christ who is the core and cornerstone of everything that we believe in and all that

---

[17] Romney, Marion G., *Look to God and Live*, General Conference, Oct. 1970.
[18] Title page, *The Book of Mormon.*

we do. The Book of Mormon plainly and powerfully testifies of the reality of Jesus Christ.

Much of the world rejects Jesus as their Savior and Redeemer. Many deny his divinity while others doubt his doctrine. But the Book of Mormon, in its clear and distinctive dialect, declares the truth of the divine mission and perfect life of our Lord and Savior.

"There is a God," declares Nephi, *"and he is Christ."* [19]

The Book of Mormon elucidates Christ's sacred teachings and holy doctrines; it testifies of his atoning sacrifice. There can be no doubt that the Book of Mormon is an essential and necessary keystone in affirming to the world that Jesus is the Christ, the Eternal God.

- **The Keystone of Our Personal Faith**

Besides being the keystone of our religion, the Book of Mormon should also be an essential keystone of our personal faith. A greater understanding of the Book of Mormon will help to secure our faith in Jesus Christ. President Ezra Taft Benson acknowledged: *"I have noted within the Church the difference in discernment,*

---

[19] 2 Nephi 11:7.

in insight, conviction, and spirit between those who know and love the Book of Mormon and those who do not. That book is a great sifter." [20]

President Ezra Taft Benson [21] further outlined the testimony of the Savior himself declaring that:

- *The Book of Mormon is true,* [22]
- *It contains the word of God,* [23]
- *It was translated by power from on high,* [24]
- *It contains the fullness of the gospel of Jesus Christ,* [25]
- *It was given by inspiration and confirmed by the ministering of angels,* [26]
- *It gives evidence that the holy scriptures are true,* [27] *and*

---

[20] Benson, Ezra Taft, *New Era*, May 1975, p. 19.

[21] Benson, Ezra Taft, *A Witness and a Warning*, Deseret Book, Salt Lake City, Utah, 1988, p. 15.

[22] D&C 17:6.

[23] D&C 19:26.

[24] D&C 20:8.

[25] D&C 20:9, 42:12.

[26] D&C 20:10.

[27] D&C 20:11.

- *Those who receive it in faith shall receive eternal life.* [28]

Another essential element of the Book of Mormon is that it stands as the keystone of our doctrine.

• The Keystone of Our Doctrine

The prophet Joseph Smith acknowledged: *"Take away the Book of Mormon and the revelations and where is our religion? We have none."* [29] For this reason alone, the Book of Mormon is a crucial keystone to our doctrine.

In ordinary language and easy to understand terminology, the Book of Mormon clarifies and illuminates all the essential doctrine necessary for our salvation. The Savior himself has proclaimed that the Book of Mormon contains the *"fulness of the gospel of Jesus Christ."* [30] The Book of Mormon increases our understanding and knowledge of vital principles and doctrines which are essential to our redemption.

---

[28] D&C 20:14.

[29] Smith, Joseph, *History of The Church of Jesus Christ of Latter-day Saints*, vol. 2, p.52.

[30] D&C 20:9.

The Book of Mormon is also a critical keystone in our personal testimonies of the work of the restoration.

- **The Keystone of Our Testimony**

It is an inarguable fact that The Church of Jesus Christ of Latter-day Saints stands or falls with the truthfulness of the Book of Mormon. If the Book of Mormon is suspect, then so is the prophet Joseph Smith, the deposition of modern-day revelation and the restoration of priesthood keys and authority.

The Book of Mormon was written to convince us *"that Jesus is the Christ."* [31] If your soul is searching for a more profound witness of the divinity of our Savior, if you harbor any doubts or question any aspect of your testimony of the restored gospel, read the Book of Mormon. Ponder its message. Pray about its precepts.

The Book of Mormon is a powerful testifier of truth. It is a profound conversion tool. Above all else, you will *"get nearer to God by abiding by its precepts, than by any other book."* [32]

As you are brought to a realization of the truthfulness of the Book of Mormon, you will also come

---

[31] Title Page, *Book of Mormon.*

[32] Smith, Joseph, *History of The Church of Jesus Christ of Latter-day Saints,* vol. 4, p.461.

to know that Joseph Smith is the prophet of the Restoration and that The Church of Jesus Christ of Latter-day Saints is directed today by a living prophet.

In 1941, President Heber J. Grant affirmed that *"experimental knowledge is the very best knowledge in the world; and any man who will believe what he is told to believe, in one of the closing paragraphs of the Book of Mormon, and who, after reading it, will ask God for a knowledge of its divinity, and live worthily of that knowledge will receive it."* [33]

The incredible conversion power of the Book of Mormon makes it a major keystone in our missionary efforts.

- **The Keystone of Our Missionary Labor**

Throughout the world, the Book of Mormon offers honest seekers after truth a definite verification of the restored gospel. It serves as a resounding witness of the sacred calling of the prophet Joseph Smith.

As Heber J. Grant further explains: *"I rejoice in the wonderful spirit of the Book of Mormon. I believe that it is one of the greatest missionaries in the hands of an elder that it is possible for him to have. I believe that*

---

[33] Grant, Heber J., *Gospel Standards,* 1941, p. 29.

no man can open that book and read it with a prayerful heart, and ask God, in the name of Jesus Christ, for a testimony regarding its divinity, but what the Lord will manifest unto him by His Spirit the truth of the book itself. And God has performed it; He has done it in thousands of cases. There is a mark of divinity on this book; and I maintain that no man can read [it]... without receiving an impression of this kind." [34]

Everyone who prayerfully studies the Book of Mormon can ask God if it is true and gain a testimony of its divinity. When, in answer to sincere prayer, the Holy Spirit testifies of the truthfulness of the Book of Mormon, then hearts are changed. People increase in faith and desire to unite themselves with the kingdom of God.

- **The Keystone of Our Lives**

The Book of Mormon was written for us. Ezra Taft Benson explained that the *"Nephites never had the book; neither did the Lamanites of ancient times. It was meant for us. Mormon wrote near the end of the Nephite civilization. Under the inspiration of God, who sees all things from the beginning, he abridged*

---

[34] Ibid., p. 30.

centuries of records, choosing the stories, speeches, and events that would be most helpful to us....

"'Behold, I speak unto you as if ye were present, and yet ye are not. But behold, Jesus Christ hath shown you unto me, and I know your doing.' [35]

"If they saw our day and chose those things which would be of greatest worth to us, is not that how we should study the Book of Mormon? We should constantly ask ourselves, 'Why did the Lord inspire Mormon (or Moroni or Alma) to include that in his record? What lesson can I learn from that to help me live in this day and age?'" [36]

The Book of Mormon is the keystone of our religion because it bears witness of our Savior Jesus Christ.

"Behold, I am Jesus Christ. I am the Father and the Son. In me shall all mankind have life, and that eternally." [37]

It is the keystone of our religion because it teaches pure truth. Through modern-day revelation the

---

[35] Mormon 8:34, 35.

[36] Benson, Ezra Taft, *A Witness and a Warning*, Deseret Book, Salt Lake City, Utah, 1988, pp. 19, 20.

[37] Ether 3:14.

Lord declares that the Book of Mormon contains *"the fullness of the gospel of Jesus Christ"* [38] and that *"As your Lord and your God liveth it is true."* [39] But there is something more to it than just these vital facts.

The Book of Mormon corroborates the truthfulness of the Bible. [40] It serves as verification *"to the world that the holy scriptures are true."* [41]

Its earnest objective is to provide us with the necessary principles and teachings for our eternal journey. One of the ultimate messages of the Book of Mormon, and of the Bible, is that humankind cannot reach perfection on its own.

The Apostle Paul instructs us that: *"The law was our schoolmaster to bring us unto Christ."* [42] Abinadi taught that the records maintained by the Book of Mormon prophets (including the Brass Plates of Laban) served *"to keep them in remembrance of God and their duty towards him."* [43]

---

[38] D&C 20:9.

[39] D&C 17:6.

[40] 1 Nephi 13:40.

[41] D&C 20:11.

[42] Galatians 3:24.

[43] Mosiah 13:30.

The Book of Mormon is our schoolmaster in this dispensation of time to bring us to Christ. [44] The book itself testifies that it is the holy word of God.

All scriptures are one in that they testify of Jesus. The prophet Jacob, brother of Nephi, declares that *"none of the prophets have written, nor prophesied, save they have spoken concerning this Christ."* [45]

Likewise, Nephi affirmed: *"We talk of Christ, we rejoice in Christ, we preach of Christ, we prophecy of Christ."* [46]

There is a very real and very tangible power associated with a sincere study of the Book of Mormon. As Ezra Taft Benson explains in *A Witness and A Warning*, its influence will begin to flow into our lives the moment we undertake a serious and sincere study of the truths and doctrines it contains. Our personal power to resist temptation will intensify. Our ability to elude deceptiveness will become more acute. We will

---

[44] Mosiah 13:27 – 32.

[45] Jacob 7:11.

[46] 2 Nephi 25:26.

become more adept at keeping our footing securely on the strait and narrow path. [47]

President Marion G. Romney knew of the great power present in the Book of Mormon. He attested to the blessings available for those who will read and study the Book of Mormon:

"I feel certain that if, in our homes, parents will read from the Book of Mormon prayerfully and regularly, both by themselves and with their children, the spirit of that great book will come to permeate our homes and all who dwell therein. The spirit of reverence will increase; mutual respect and consideration for each other will grow. The spirit of contention will depart. Parents will counsel their children in greater love and wisdom. Children will be more responsive and submissive to the counsel of their parents. Righteousness will increase. Faith, hope, and charity—the pure love of Christ—will abound in our homes and lives, bringing in their wake peace, joy, and happiness." [48]

The promise of increased reverence and respect in our homes, the added blessing of greater love between

---

[47] Benson, Ezra Taft, *A Witness and A Warning*, Deseret Book, Salt Lake City, Utah, 1988, pp. 21, 22.

[48] Romney, Marion G., *Ensign*, May 1980, p. 67.

parents and their children, as well as increased peace, joy and happiness are not imaginary inferences. They are, instead, precisely what Joseph Smith meant when he declared that the Book of Mormon will draw us nearer to God.

As President Benson explains: *"The scriptures are called 'the words of life,'* [49] *and nowhere is that more true than it is of the Book of Mormon. When you begin to hunger and thirst after those words, you will find life in greater and greater abundance."* [50]

---

[49] D&C 84:85

[50] Benson, Ezra Taft, *A Witness and A Warning*, Deseret Book, Salt Lake City, Utah, 1988, p. 22.

Promise 1

Nearer to God

"I told the brethren that the Book of Mormon was the most correct of any book on earth, and the keystone of our religion, and a man would get nearer to God by abiding by its precepts, than by any other book." [51]

When asked his opinion of the Mormons, Charles Dickens scoffed: *"Imagine seeing angels in the age of locomotives!"* [52] From locomotives to automobiles to

---

[51] Smith, Joseph, *History of The Church of Jesus Christ of Latter-day Saints*, vol. 4, p.461.

[52] Charles Dickens later changed his opinion of the Mormons after meeting with a group of emigrants sailing out of England for the Great Salt Lake Valley. Concerning these people, Dickens wrote: "I went on board their ship to bear testimony against them if they

airplanes to deep space exploration, we have progressively moved into an age of extensive and illustrious enlightenment. Humanity is making unprecedented progress in countless fields, spheres and disciplines. Inventions that were, at one time, nothing more than the wild imaginings of science-fiction writers have become commonplace today.

In his book, *The Progress of Man*, Joseph Fielding Smith writes: *"Great progress has been made in mechanics, chemistry, physics, surgery, and other things. Men have built great telescopes that have brought the hidden galaxies to view. They have, by the aid of the microscope, discovered vast worlds of microorganisms, some of which are as deadly as are men towards their fellow men. They have discovered means to control disease; they have, by the aid of anesthesia, made men insensible to pain, thus permitting major and delicate operations which could*

---

deserved it, as I fully believed they would; to my great astonishment they did not deserve it." After observing and mingling with the converts, Dickens was impressed with them and described these English converts as being "the pick and flower of England." (See Charles Dickens, *"The Uncommercial Traveler,"* All the Year Round, July 4, 1863, 449; see also David M. W. Pickup, *The Pick and Flower of England* (2001).

not otherwise be performed. They have invented machines more sensitive than the human touch, more far-seeing than the human eye. They have controlled elements and made machinery that can move mountains, and many other things have they done too numerous to mention. Yes, this is a wonderful age. However, all of these discoveries and inventions have not drawn men nearer to God!" [53]

With all our discoveries and advancements in technology, science and education, faith has not increased in the world. Obedience to God has become arbitrary instead of obligatory. Righteousness does not rule our beliefs or our behaviors. Perhaps more now than in any other age of society, humanity needs to draw nearer to God.

In the Memorial Chapel at Stanford University we find these words: *"There is no narrowing so deadly as the narrowing of man's horizon of spiritual things. No worse evil could befall him in his course on earth than to lose sight of heaven; and it is not civilization that can prevent this; it is not civilization that can compensate for it. No widening of science, no possession of abstract truth, can indemnify for an*

---

[53] Smith, Joseph Fielding, *The Progress of Man*, Deseret Book Company, 1936.

enfeebled hold on the highest and eternal truth of humanity."

What an enormous blessing and benefit it would be for the world to acquire a deeper abiding faith in our Redeemer and a greater love in our hearts toward each other! If we would enlighten our spirits with the same intensity that we have enlightened our minds and turn to the Lord, we could have the confidence that he will be near, that he will help us fight our battles and fill our lives with the principles of truth and righteousness.

In speaking about the Book of Mormon, Ezra Taft Benson has challenged all of us to *"prayerfully consider steps that we can personally take to bring this new witness for Christ more fully into our own lives and into a world that so desperately needs it.... I have a vision of the whole Church getting nearer to God by abiding by the precepts of the Book of Mormon. Indeed, I have a vision of flooding the earth with the Book of Mormon."* [54]

What the world most needs today is to draw nearer to God. Anyone who has viewed and studied the Book of Mormon with more than just a casual pursuing knows the truthfulness of the prophet Joseph Smith's

---

[54] Benson, Ezra Taft, *Flooding the Earth with the Book of Mormon,* The Ensign, November 1988, p. 4.

assertion. The Book of Mormon will draw us nearer to God. It is a meaningful and inspired declaration of him and an additional witness and testament of our Savior Jesus Christ.

Promise 2

Manifest the Truth

"Behold, I would exhort you that when ye shall read these things, if it be wisdom in God that ye should read them, that ye would remember how merciful the Lord hath been unto the children of men, from the creation of Adam even down until the time that ye shall receive these things, and ponder it in your hearts.

"And when ye shall receive these things, I would exhort you that ye would ask God, the Eternal Father, in the name of Christ, if these things are not true; and if ye shall ask with a sincere heart, with real intent, having faith in Christ, he will manifest the truth of it unto you, by the power of the Holy Ghost." [55]

---

[55] Moroni 10:3,4.

I have noticed a special power associated with the Book of Mormon. A quiet, yet convincing witness of its truth is conveyed to those who delve into its pages with faith and a sincere intent.

Parley P. Pratt stated: *"The Spirit of the Lord came upon me, while I read, and enlightened my mind, convinced my judgment, and riveted the truth upon my understanding, so that I knew that the book was true, just as well as a man knows the daylight from the dark night."* [56]

Paul teaches that: *"The things of God knoweth no man, but the Spirit of God."* [57] The truthfulness of the Book of Mormon is manifest to every sincere seeker by the power of the Holy Ghost. God will not allow our faith to go unrewarded. His promise to us is that *"signs shall follow them that believe."* [58] These signs will serve as evidences of truth which confirm that our faith is not in vain.

Brigham Young experienced this marvelous blessing as he read the Book of Mormon: *"I knew it was true, as well as I knew that I could see with my eyes, or*

---

[56] *Journal of Discourses* 5:194.
[57] 1 Corinthians 2:11.
[58] Mark 16:17.

feel by the touch of my fingers, or be sensible of the demonstration of any sense." [59]

Moroni's promise provides us an explicit procedure for gaining a testimony, not only of the Book of Mormon, but of all spiritual truth. The formula applies to those seeking a witness of the truthfulness of the Book of Mormon and is also the process for hearing the voice of the Lord every time we read from its inspired pages.

We should ponder and pray with faith and real intent not only the first time we read the Book of Mormon and not only when we are seeking a spiritual witness of its truthfulness. We should ponder and pray every time we read it. Doing so will enable us to receive a greater testimony and a *"more sure witness"* from the Lord.

To ascertain truth in the spiritual realm we must ask God. *"Ask, and it shall be given you,"* [60] but *"ask in faith, nothing wavering."* [61] If we will be humble and pray sincerely, with real intent, with faith in Christ, doubting nothing, He will manifest to us the truth we are seeking by the power of the Holy Ghost. He will tell

---

[59] *Journal of Discourses* 3:91.
[60] Matthew 7:7.
[61] James 1:6.

us what we want to know. The Lord assures us a firm witness of the truth by the power of the Holy Ghost.

"It is the Spirit that beareth witness, because the Spirit is truth." [62]

---

[62] 1 John 5:6.

Promise 3

Delicious to Me

"Now, we will compare the word unto a seed. Now, if ye give place, that a seed may be planted in your heart, behold, if it be a true seed, or a good seed, if ye do not cast it out by your unbelief, that ye will resist the Spirit of the Lord, behold, it will begin to swell within your breasts; and when you feel these swelling motions, ye will begin to say within yourselves—It must needs be that this is a good seed, or that the word is good, for it beginneth to enlarge my soul; yea, it beginneth to enlighten my understanding, yea, it beginneth to be delicious to me." [63]

---

[63] Alma 32:28.

Much like music and art, the Book of Mormon reveals a whole new world to us. We become associated with God's law and live in harmony with correct gospel teachings. Our religious belief moves beyond mere duty to something akin to passion. It creates in us a hungering and thirsting after righteousness that must be filled.

The quest for truth is essentially an experiment upon the words of Christ. The experimenter is encouraged to *"prove all things; hold fast that which is good."* [64]

Comparing this religious fervor to a fruit tree, Alma promises us that *"ye shall pluck the fruit thereof, which is most precious, which is sweet above all that is sweet, and which is white above all that is white, yea, and pure above all that is pure; and ye shall feast upon this fruit even until ye are filled, that ye hunger not, neither shall ye thirst."* [65]

Lehi envisioned the fruit of the tree of life as filling his soul *"with exceedingly great joy"* and that *"it was desirable above all other fruit."* [66]

---

[64] 1 Thessalonians 5:21.
[65] Alma 32:42.
[66] 1 Nephi 8:12.

From a similar vision, Joseph Smith, Sr. described the fruit of the tree as *"delicious beyond description...*

"The more we ate," he explains, *"the more we seemed to desire, until we even got down upon our knees and scooped it up, eating it by double handfuls."* [67]

In his book, *Living by the Power of Faith*, Gene R. Cook asks:

"How do you correctly recognize that feeling and know that the seed (the word) is from God? Alma gives three definite evidences that tell you if the seed comes from the Lord:

"1. It begins to enlarge your soul.

"2. It begins to enlighten your understanding.

"3. It begins to be delicious to you." [68]

---

[67] Smith, Lucy Mack, *History of Joseph Smith by His Mother.* Deseret Book Company, 1979. Pp. 49, 50.

[68] Cook, Gene R., *Living by the Power of Faith*. Deseret Book Company, 1985.

This is the beginning of true faith. It is an introduction to the fruits of the Spirit. In his epistle to the Galatians, Paul enumerates the fruits of religion:

"But the fruit of the Spirit is love, joy, peace, long suffering, gentleness, goodness, faith, meekness, temperance; against such there is no law." [69]

The apostle Peter also wrote:

"Giving all diligence, add to your faith virtue; and to virtue knowledge; and to knowledge temperance, and to temperance patience; and to patience godliness; and to godliness brotherly kindness; and to brotherly kindness, charity. For if these things be in you, and abound, they make you that ye shall neither be barren nor unfruitful in the knowledge of our Lord Jesus Christ." [70]

It is evident from these inspired writings that the fruits of the Spirit are to be realized and savored in our present earth life as well as in our eternal life. These spiritual gifts are offered to us today, as well as tomorrow.

The Book of Mormon will live in our hearts and in our lives when we begin to delight in the word of God.

---

[69] Galatians 5:22,23.
[70] 2 Peter 1:5-8.

Then we will become true disciples of Christ, realizing the destiny described so articulately by President Ezra Taft Benson: "*I have a vision of homes alerted, classes alive, pulpits aflame, with the spirit of the Book of Mormon message. I have a vision of the whole church getting nearer to God by abiding by the precepts of the Book of Mormon.*" [71]

Our religious convictions will not shelter us from all sorrow and suffering, nor do they promise us a life of prosperity, but they do assure us the precious fruits of the spirit—peace, joy, love, and a purposeful life.

---

[71] Benson, Ezra Taft, General Conference, Oct. 1988.

Promise 4

Prepare a Way

"And it came to pass that I, Nephi, said unto my father: I will go and do the things which the Lord hath commanded, for I know that the Lord giveth no commandments unto the children of men, save he shall prepare a way for them that they may accomplish the thing which he commandeth them." [72]

Nephi's example and teaching from the preceding verse are essential for any member of the Church seeking reassurance of the basic rudiments of gospel

---

[72] 1 Nephi 3:7.

living with its encumbrance of daily taking up the cross of Christ and following Him.[73]

In writing about heroes from the Book of Mormon, Russel M. Nelson tells us that *"Nephi was a multifaceted genius. Endowed with great physical stature, he was a prophet, teacher, ruler, colonizer, builder, craftsman, scholar, writer, poet, military leader, and father of nations. Nephi had a sincere desire to know the mysteries of God. He became a special witness and trusted prophet of the Lord... Appropriately, his final testimony closed with the words that could be known as his signature: 'I must obey.'"* [74]

Very few prophets of the past have spoken with such genuine intensity to the denizens of our day. Nephi's life, calling and dedication to the Lord were destined to be a blessing not only to his own people but to generations and generations of God's children.

Like Nephi, the Apostle Paul also reassures us:

"There hath no temptation taken you but such as is common to man: but God is faithful, who will not

---

[73] See Luke 9:23.

[74] Nelson, Russel M., *Heroes from the Book of Mormon*, Deseret Book Company, 1995.

suffer you to be tempted above that ye are able; but will with the temptation also make a way to escape, that ye may be able to bear it." [75]

Our Heavenly Father loves all his children. He wants to guide and direct us along paths of peace and safety. He also understands that we cannot be guided in arrogance or directed in pride. When we are enduring the tests and trials of our lifetimes, when things just aren't going well, we can and should understand that our loving Father is leading us through life experiences that will both bless and better us. With the prayer of faith and a determination to obey, we can recognize what the Lord requires of us and be assured that the way has already been prepared for us.

Henry B. Eyring has challenged us that when we are experiencing a severe trial, we should ask ourselves the following question:

"'Am I trying to do what the Lord would have me do?' If you're not, then adjust your course. But if you are, remember the boy outside the walls of Jerusalem who... said, 'I will go and do the things which the Lord hath commanded, for I know that the Lord giveth no commandments unto the children of men, save he

---

[75] 1 Corinthians 10:13.

shall prepare a way for them that they may accomplish the thing which he commandeth them.'" [76]

No obstacle in life is insurmountable when God commands and we obey. President Eyring continues:

"The Lord will always prepare a way for you to escape from the trials you will be given if you understand two things. One is that you need to be on the Lord's errand. The second thing you need to understand is that the escape will almost never be out of the trial; it will usually be through it. If you pray to have the experience removed altogether, you may not find the way prepared for you. Instead, you need to pray to find the way of deliverance through it." [77]

Joseph F. Smith assures us that if *"the Latter-day Saints are content to obey the commandments of God... our heavenly Father is bound by his oath and covenant to protect them from every opposing foe, and to help them to overcome every obstacle that can possible be arrayed against them, or thrown in their pathway."* [78]

---

[76] Eyring, Henry B., *To Draw Closer to God*, Deseret Book Company, 1997.
[77] Ibid.
[78] Smith, Joseph F., General Conference, April 1883. JD 24:176.

Whoever we are and no matter how difficult our situation, the Book of Mormon offers us the reassurance that whatever our Father commands us to do to qualify for the blessings of eternal life, it will not be beyond our capacity to obey.

Promise 5

Humble are Blessed

"Yea, he that truly humbleth himself, and repenteth of his sins, and endureth to the end, the same shall be blessed--yea, much more blessed than they who are compelled to be humble because of their exceeding poverty." [79]

Jesus began the Sermon on the Mount by specifying eight stipulations for human happiness, the third being *"Blessed are the meek."* [80] The term meek has customarily implied being humble, free of pride and

---

[79] Alma 32:15.
[80] Matthew 5:5.

arrogance. David O. McKay referred to humility as *"the solid foundation of all the virtues."* [81]

Humanity disdains the quality and characteristic of the humble and meek, but Jesus describes humility as the distinctive trait of his disciples. It is one of the greatest Christian virtues. Submissiveness to God is not a weakness but an eternal quality of the faithful. King Benjamin portrayed the humble and submissive as yielding *"to the enticings of the Holy Spirit."* A humble follower of Christ *"putteth off the natural man and becometh a saint through the atonement of Christ the Lord, and becometh as a child, submissive, meek, humble, patient, full of love, willing to submit to all things which the Lord seeth fit to inflict upon him, even as a child doth submit to his father."* [82]

The world does not place humility high on its list of desirable attributes. The humble are most often viewed as compliant and cowardly, timid and retiring, weak-willed and wary, submissive and subservient; attempting nothing, accomplishing nothing, and adding nothing to society. These false worldly views should not dissuade us from developing this attribute that the Savior himself personified.

---

[81] McKay, David O., *Ancient Apostles*, p. 118.
[82] Mosiah 3:19.

Humility is an attribute of those with a healthy sense of self-worth. Being sensitive to shortcomings and aware of our weaknesses is essential to our personal growth and progress. Self-esteem and self-conceit are counterparts, not equivalences.

The humble submit themselves to the will of God and find increased strength and greater power. We should develop humility simply because God commands us to be humble but the blessings of being humble clarify also our constant need for this Christian virtue. Some of the benefits of being humble are specifically outlined in the scriptures.

The Lord *"shall lead thee by the hand, and give thee answer to thy prayers."* [83]

The Lord's grace is sufficient for the humble and he will *"make weak things become strong unto them."* [84]

The humble will be made strong and *"receive knowledge from time to time."* [85]

---

[83] D&C 112:10.
[84] See Ether 12:26,27.
[85] See D&C 1:28.

The spirit will be sent to enlighten those who are humble. [86]

The *"ignorant"* will *"learn wisdom by humbling himself."* [87]

The *"veil shall be rent"* and the humble will see and know the Lord. [88]

No one can assist in the work of the Lord *"except he shall be humble."* [89]

The pragmatic appeal of personal humility is in its ability to notice a failing and accept the instruction and consequent correction that come from that failing. Humility is the indispensable element in improvement and personal growth, despite mistakes and disappointments. Progress, whether in business, education, religion, or elsewhere is accelerated when we quickly and humbly learn from our mistakes and failures.

The humble are teachable and open-minded. They are taught by their contemporaries as well as by God because they are not concerned with their own

---

[86] See D&C 136:33.

[87] D&C 136:32.

[88] See D&C 67:10.

[89] See D&C 12:8.

self-image and self-importance and can truly listen and learn. As humble followers of Christ, they recognize that there is a standard of perfection to be pursued.

Pride, on the other hand, disconnects us from God and disengages us from others. Pride deadens our sense of relationship with our Father in heaven. It dictates that *"my will,"* not *"thine,"* be done.

Pride wears many guises. It ascends in the arrogance of the academic and parades in the pompousness of the prosperous. It hides in the hypocrisy of the self-righteous and struts in the sanctimoniousness of the socialite.

The proud isolate themselves from others. Grateful that they are *"not as other men are,"* [90] they shun sympathy, compassion and kindness toward others. The humble, on the other hand, abandon arrogance and accept that in God's guidelines there can be no constraint on love.

The love Jesus exemplified is boundless. He despised the self-importance and presumptuousness of the Pharisees. They perform *"all their deeds to be seen by people, for they make their phylacteries wide*

---

[90] Luke 18:11.

and their tassels long. They love the place of honor at banquets and the best seats in the synagogues and elaborate greetings in the market place." [91] Conceivably the most treacherous characteristic of their conceit was that they saw themselves as not needing repentance. [92] But of us, Christ invites a profound, personal, and positive humility that will collapse our conceit and dissolve the defenses between us and God and between us and all of humanity.

Elder Bruce R. McConkie wrote: *"As things are now constituted, the meek do not inherit the earth; even He who said of himself, 'I am meek and lowly of heart'* [93] *had in fact no place of his own to lay his head. This world's goods were of little moment to him, and he had neither gold nor silver nor houses nor lands nor kingdoms. Peter was even directed to catch a fish in whose mouth a coin was lodged, that a levied tax might be paid for the two of them. The meek—those who are the God-fearing and the righteous—seldom hold title to much of that which appertains to this present world. But there will be a day when the Lord shall come to*

---

[91] Matthew 23:5-7 (NET).

[92] See Luke 15:1-7.

[93] Matthew 11:29.

make up his jewels; there will be a day when Abraham, Isaac, and Jacob, and the faithful of ancient Israel shall dwell again in old Canaan; and there will be also an eventual celestial day when 'the poor and the meek of the earth shall inherit it.'" [94] [95]

The day will soon come when eternal principles will prevail on earth. What humanity despises today will eventually be acknowledged and appreciated as an essential attribute of a righteous and Christ-like character.

_____

[94] D&C 88:17.
[95] McConkie, Bruce R., *The Mortal Messiah*, vol. 2, p. 122. Deseret Book Company.

Promise 6

Claim on Mercy

"Therefore, whosoever repenteth, and hardeneth not his heart, he shall have claim on mercy through mine Only Begotten Son, unto a remission of his sins; and these shall enter into my rest." [96]

Our earthly experiences have been described as a *"life amid broken harmonies."* [97] These broken harmonies, with the rich lessons and essential experiences they provide, are possible only as a result of disobedience to law through the fall of Adam. Adam's transgression initiated our life on earth and provided us with the

---

[96] Alma 12:34.

[97] Roberts, B.H., *Seventy's Course in Theology*, vol. 4, Deseret Book Company, 1911.

circumstances necessary for our instruction, which include the *"broken harmonies"* of good versus evil; faith versus doubt; hope versus despair; joy versus sorrow; pleasure versus pain; life versus death. With Adam's transgression, the circumstances and conditions required for our earthly education and subsequent eternal progression were formed. Furthermore, each of us sins of our own accord and incurs the consequence of wrongdoing. In either case, we are incapable of reinstating what has been lost or creating a justification for forgiveness in our fallen state.

This creates a condition remedied in only one of two ways: Justice must be obtained, and punishment exacted on the actual sinner or God must fulfill the claim against us, appeasing justice through a vicarious atonement on our behalf. The first possibility would prevent the purposes of God from unfolding and would violate our promise for eternal life. The second option is the only valid alternative. God must appease the demands of justice, allowing mercy to establish its claims and redeem a fallen humanity.

The apostle Paul instructs us that: *"By grace are ye saved through faith; and that not of yourselves; it is the gift of God.*

"The law entered that sin might abound. But where sin abounded, grace did more abound; that as sin hath reigned unto death, even so might grace reign through righteousness, unto eternal life by Jesus Christ our Lord." [98]

Underlying this gift of grace is God's boundless love for us manifest in his tender mercy; mercy which is simply love in action. God's love for us prompts him to satisfy justice by enduring the penalty due to Adam's sin. God's love for us prompts him to suffer for the individual sins of humanity; to exact the price of each person's sin. This love prescribes the sinner's claim on mercy.

That is the gospel, the great plan of happiness. That is the *"good tidings of great joy, which shall be unto all people."* [99]

Jesus Christ is the personification of mercy and mercy is the essence of the gospel of Jesus Christ. Our Savior's sacrifice on the cross was an unparalleled act of mercy on our behalf. His earthly ministry encompassed compassion toward the needy and neglected, the ill and the infirm and the disheartened and downtrodden. The extent of compassion that we

---

[98] Romans 5:20,21.
[99] Luke 2:10.

extend to others is the expression of our distinct discipleship to our Redeemer.

"Our salvation," wrote Harold B. Lee, *"rests upon the mercy we show to others. Unkind and cruel words, or wanton acts of cruelty toward man or beast, even though in seeming retaliation, disqualify the perpetrator in his claims for mercy when he has need of mercy in the day of judgment before earthly or heavenly tribunals.... Blessed are all you who are merciful, for you shall obtain mercy!"* [100]

King Benjamin suggested that we are all beggars, dependent upon God for all the *"substance which we have, for both food and raiment, and for gold, and for silver, and for all the riches which we have of every kind...*

"And now," he declares, *"if God, who has created you, on whom you are dependent for your lives and for all that ye have and are, doth grant unto you whatsoever ye ask that is right... O then, how ye ought to impart of the substance that ye have one to another."* [101]

---

[100] Lee, Harold B., *Stand Ye in Holy Places*, Deseret Book, p. 346.
[101] See Mosiah 4:19, 21.

Mercy is not the disposition of the arrogant, the conceited or the self-centered. If we expect a claim on mercy, our nature must be one of compassion, gentleness, kindness, patience and respect toward others.

Bruce R. McConkie recognized that mercy is a reward reserved for the merciful. *"In that great day of restoration and judgment,"* he wrote, *"when every man is rewarded according to the deeds done in the flesh, those who have manifest mercy to their fellowmen here will be treated mercifully by the Merciful One. Those who have acquired the godly attribute of mercy here shall have mercy restored unto them again in that bright day."* [102]

As we learn to become more merciful, compassionate, gentler and kinder, we will earn a greater claim on mercy from God who will be generous in his mercy toward us.

---

[102] McConkie, Bruce R., *The Mortal Messiah*, vol. 2, pp. 122, 123. Deseret Book Company.

Promise 7

The Lord Will Hear Us

"Yea, thou art merciful unto thy children when they cry unto thee, to be heard of thee and not of men, and thou wilt hear them." [103]

Latter-day Saints are expected to be diligent in prayer, both in private and with our families. The purpose of prayer is to allow us to communicate with our Father in heaven and have a medium open between us and God through which we can solicit blessings from heaven. Genuine prayer is articulated in the sincere feelings and supplications emerging from a broken and humble

---

[103] Alma 33:8.

heart. It stems from an inward appeal to seek in faith the blessings of a loving father.

When we do not practice the process of prayer, we deny ourselves the light and inspiration of his Spirit. We forego the feelings of gratitude that should fill our hearts and we disavow the desire to praise God for his goodness and mercy toward us.

Not only are we *expected* to pray but we are *entitled* to pray and ask of our Father for all things, whether temporal or spiritual, that we rightfully need. Modern-day revelation states: *"Ye are commanded in all things to ask of God."* [104] The Lord's Prayer teaches us that we should ask for *"our daily bread."* [105] James urges us to seek wisdom. [106] Amulek advises us to pray over crops and herds, over fields and flocks, as well as for mercy and salvation.[107] Nephi admonishes us that we *"must not perform any thing unto the Lord save in the first place ye shall pray unto the Father in the name of Christ, that he will consecrate thy performance unto*

---

[104] D&C 46:7.
[105] Matthew 6:11.
[106] James 1:5.
[107] See Alma 34:17-29.

thee, that thy performance may be for the welfare of thy soul." [108]

Clearly, we are expected to pray for all that we righteously and prudently need or desire. The Lord has promised the faithful: *"If thou shalt ask, thou shalt receive...."* [109] This does not, of course, give us the right to unwise and unlimited petition. All our requests must be based on righteous desires, and not on selfish greed or lust. As the apostle James explains: *"Ye ask, and receive not, because ye ask amiss, that ye may consume it upon your lusts."* [110]

We should seek for the gifts of the Spirit. We should plead for a more powerful testimony. We should ask for personal revelation. Most importantly, we should solicit the companionship of the Holy Ghost. When the Nephite apostles prayed, they *"desired that the Holy Ghost be given unto them."* [111] One of the greatest gift we can receive in this life is the gift of the Holy Ghost. [112]

---

[108] 2 Nephi 32:9.
[109] D&C 42:61.
[110] James 4:3.
[111] 3 Nephi 19:9.
[112] See D&C 14:7.

There may be times when it seems that the heavens are closed to us and that the Lord does not answer our prayers despite the promise that *"whatsoever thing ye shall ask in prayer, believing, ye shall receive."* [113] A careful examination may reveal the reasons for this seeming contradiction.

Prayers we thought were unheard and unanswered may have been answered through spiritual promptings and feelings that went unrecognized because we were insensitive to them.

Answers may be delayed because God wants us to study, search and ponder more before he responds.

It could be that God is simply waiting for us to decide first before confirming that decision through the Spirit.

God will always respect our free agency as well as our spiritual knowledge and understanding. Sometimes he allows us to decide and act for ourselves.

On the other hand, God may postpone a response if we are too spiritually immature to acknowledge or accept his answer.

---

[113] Matthew 21:7.

Some prayers go unanswered because they are simply contrary to the will of God.

We should always be patient and remember that we may not receive an answer to our prayers until our faith and perseverance have been tried and tested. Instead of questioning or losing faith in God over seemingly unanswered prayers, we should evaluate our own intentions and purposes when praying and strive to develop a deeper spiritual sensitivity to the voice of the Spirit.

In his book, *Receiving Answers to Our Prayers*, Gene R. Cook assures us that:

"1. God listens to our prayers and answers them. [114] *I believe there has not been one sincere prayer offered by any man since the 'beginning' that has gone unanswered.*

"2. God lives and loves us and will give correct answers to all sincere prayers, no matter what the question is. [115]

---

[114] See D&C 98:2, 3; 88:2.
[115] See Moroni 10:4, 5.

"3. We are children of God and servants of the Lord. We can pray as Samuel did: 'Speak; for thy servant heareth.' [116]

"4. It doesn't matter how old we are, or what our church position is, or how long we've been members of the Church. The Lord desires to answer our sincere requests regardless of these things." [117]

Sincere prayer, practiced on a regular, consistent basis, is the most prevailing and influential force for putting us on the path of spiritual development and for keeping us on the narrow road to righteousness. The rewards of honest and purposeful prayer will be an inexpressible sustenance to our souls.

---

[116] 1 Samuel 3:10.

[117] Cook, Gene R., *Receiving Answers to Our Prayers*, Deseret Book Company, Salt Lake City, UT 1996.

Promise 8

Guiltless Before God

"And now, for the sake of these things which I have spoken unto you—that is, for the sake of retaining a remission of your sins from day to day, that ye may walk guiltless before God—I would that ye should impart of your substance to the poor, every man according to that which he hath, such as feeding the hungry, clothing the naked, visiting the sick and administering to their relief, both spiritually and temporally, according to their wants." [118]

No one walks through this life blameless. Jesus Christ was the only perfect being to ever grace this planet. He committed no sin during his lifetime and never strayed

---

[118] Mosiah 4:26.

from the path of righteousness. Despite our imperfections, this one perfect person, through the Book of Mormon, promises us that if we will strive to remain free from sin and attend to the needs and sufferings of others, he will remit our wrongdoing and declare us guiltless at the last day.

We are all beholden to someone. We are indebted to our earthly parents for our birth and for sustaining our lives until we could do so on our own. Likewise, we are indebted to our Savior for preparing a passageway from the grave to a glorious resurrection as well as for his atonement for our sins. Not one of us can orchestrate our salvation on our own.

Every life that ever appeared on this earth has been enriched by someone other than itself. All of us have, in one sense or another, reaped where we have not sown and harvested where we did not plant.

Poverty is a universal concern that exists in every country and flourishes in every community. In countries with a lower Gross National Product, disease and deprivation, hunger and starvation, illiteracy and lack of education, crime and corruption thrive at significantly higher levels. Excessive poverty is the root cause of a multitude of humanity's difficulties and a definite display of human bondage, dependency and subjugation.

All of us are reliant on the help of someone outside of ourselves and so, all of us are obliged to offer similar blessings and benefits to others in need. Our Savior, on whom we are all dependent, taught that greatness is not found in the strength to take away, but in our ability to give away. The Greatest of all declared: *"He that is greatest among you shall be your servant."* [119] There is no true greatness without service.

George F. Richards affirmed that: *"The Lord expects us when he blesses us with the good things of this earth to remember those who are not so fortunate. We are to feed the hungry, clothe the naked, visit the sick, comfort those who mourn, and minister unto those who are poor and needy, and thus become of that class to whom the Lord, when he shall come, shall say: 'Come, ye blessed of the Father, inherit the kingdom prepared for you from the foundation of the world.'"* [120]

King Benjamin eloquently outlined our divine duty and commission to offer aid and relief to others, imparting with them what we have been abundantly given from God. [121] We may question, however, the

---

[119] Matthew 23:11.

[120] Richards, George F., *Conference Report*, October 1939, pp. 108-109.

[121] See Mosiah 4.

wisdom of giving to those who, like Alfred P. Doolittle in *My Fair Lady*, are *"the undeserving poor."* Fortunately for us, we have no divine duty or commission to sit in judgment of others and to neglect our responsibility to share and to serve anyone in need demonstrates an ungodly selfishness which places our own salvation in peril.

Marion G. Romney made clear the key element that will allow us to walk guiltless before God: *"In this modern world plagued with counterfeits for the Lord's plan, we must not be misled into supposing that we can discharge our obligations to the poor and the needy by shifting the responsibility to some governmental or other public agency. Only by voluntarily giving out of an abundant love for our neighbors can we develop that charity characterized by Mormon as 'the pure love of Christ.'* [122] *This we must develop if we would obtain eternal life."* [123]

Caring for others in need is not merely our Christian responsibility. It extends beyond the ordinary obligation of a disciple of Christ. It is an honored opportunity to do something in return for the one Solitary Soul who did for us what we could not do for

---

[122] Moroni 7:47.

[123] Romney, Marion G., *Conference Report*, October 1972, p. 115.

ourselves. Whatever we do *"unto one of the least of these,"* [124] we do also to him. Caring for the needy is an indisputable indication that the Spirit of the Lord is existent among us.

"The Lord doesn't really need us to take care of the poor," explained Marion G. Romney. *"He could take care of them without our help if it were his purpose to do so. 'I, the Lord,' he said, 'stretched out the heavens, and built the earth, my very handiwork; and all things therein are mine.*

"'And it is my purpose to provide for my saints, for all things are mine.' [125]

".... No, the Lord doesn't really need us to care for the poor, but we need this experience; for it is only through our learning how to take care of each other that we develop within us the Christlike love and disposition necessary to qualify us to return to his presence." [126]

He further reminds us that *"you cannot give yourself poor in this work; you can only give yourself*

---

[124] Matthew 25:40.

[125] D&C 104:14, 15.

[126] Romney, Marion G., *Conference Report*, October 1981, pp. 130-131.

rich. I have satisfied myself regarding the truthfulness of the statement made to me by Elder Melvin J. Ballard as he set me apart for my mission in 1920: 'A person cannot give a crust to the Lord without receiving a loaf in return.'

"The Savior taught that it is more blessed to give than to receive. [127] *Through church welfare, both the giver and the receiver are blessed in unique ways--each to the sanctification and salvation of his eternal soul."* [128]

It has been said that attending to the needs of the poor is an expression of the greatest gift and the most Christian characteristic, the attitude of charity. [129] It is, simply put, a service we offer to God. [130]

From the *Commentary on the Book of Mormon* we discover that it *"is indisputable that 'feeding the hungry, clothing the naked, visiting the sick and administering to their relief, both spiritually and temporally' renders us more obedient to God's commandments and thereby creates in us a clean*

---

[127] See Acts 20:35.

[128] Romney, Marion G., *Conference Report*, October 1980, p. 130.

[129] See 1 Corinthians 13:13.

[130] See Matthew 25:31-40, Mosiah 2:17, D&C 42:38.

heart and renews a steadfast spirit within us. [131] *Doing so is a sacrifice of righteousness when, in offering it, we put our trust in the Lord. There is no surer way to remember the Lord, His goodness and mercy, than to serve His children who want and have not.*

"Blessings without number attend the giver of these things. Not only do we retain a remission of our sins, but it follows that also we may walk 'guiltless before God,' who is our loving parent." [132]

When we give freely to others in need, we are promised a wealth of blessings, including happiness, forgiveness and eternal life. Caring for others is not only a meaningful moral obligation; it is our Christian responsibility.

---

[131] See Psalms 51:10.

[132] Siodahl, Janne M. & Reynolds, George, *Commentary on the Book of Mormon,* vol. 2, Deseret Book Company, Salt Lake City, 1956.

Promise 9

Sins are Forgiven

"And there came a voice unto me, saying: Enos, thy sins are forgiven thee, and thou shalt be blessed." [133]

We have all done something that we shouldn't have done. Or perhaps, we didn't do something we should have done. In either case, we have all made mistakes and we all need to repent.

President Harold B. Lee has counseled: *"Let us confess it, all of us are 'sinners anonymous.' All of us have done things we ought not to have done, or we*

---

[133] Enos 1:5.

have neglected things we should have done; and every one of us has need for repentance." [134]

In the New Testament, John instructed that *"If we say that we have no sin, we deceive ourselves, and the truth is not in us. If we confess our sins, he is faithful and just to forgive us our sins, and to cleanse us from all unrighteousness."* [135] All of us have sinned, but there is hope in the redemption of Christ.

Enos depicted the procedure of obtaining a remission of sin as a *"wrestle... before God."* [136] Forgiveness is attained by means of the atonement of Christ. It is a gift, but it is a gift that is earned through honest, sincere changes in character and behavior. Cautioning us that *"no unclean thing can enter into his kingdom,"* the Book of Mormon acknowledges that *"nothing entereth into his rest save it be those who have washed their garments in [his] blood, because of their faith, and the repentance of all their sins, and their faithfulness unto the end."* [137]

---

[134] Lee, Harold B., *Teachings of Harold B. Lee*, Deseret Book, p. 212.
[135] 1 John 1:8, 9.
[136] Enos 1:2.
[137] 3 Nephi 27:19.

As disciples of Christ we must resolve our past sinful behavior with our current righteous desires, because all of us *"have sinned and come short of the glory of God."* [138] Essentially, we must demonstrate unfaltering faith in Christ, recognize our own unworthiness, and humbly acknowledge that he suffered and died for the sins of all the world, including our own. The initial experience of repentance and forgiveness forms the foundation for our testimony of the gospel of Jesus Christ and inspires a constant commitment to Christian living and service.

Forgiveness comes through redemption. Webster's Dictionary tells us that to redeem is to *"buy or win back,"* but it also means *"to free from distress or harm, to free from captivity by payment of ransom, to release from blame or debt, to change for the better, to help overcome something detrimental, to free from the consequence of sin."* [139] Each of these definitions aptly applies to the redemption Christ offers his faithful followers. In his epistle to the Ephesians, Paul employs the term *"accepted."*

"To the praise of the glory of his grace," writes the apostle, *"wherein he hath made us accepted in the*

---

[138] Romans 3:23.

[139] www.merriam-webster.com/dictionary/redeem.

beloved. *In whom we have redemption through his blood, the forgiveness of sins, according to the riches of his grace."* [140] We are received and accepted by the Redeemer as we receive and accept him into our hearts and lives. His redemption accomplishes our forgiveness.

The qualifying condition for forgiveness placed on us is that we must extend to all humanity the same grace that we so freely receive. Christ our Redeemer proclaimed: *"For, if ye forgive men their trespasses your heavenly Father will also forgive you; But if ye forgive not men their trespasses neither will your Father forgive your trespasses."* [141] No mention is made of whether the offenders deserve our forgiveness or not.

Expressed words of forgiveness toward others without a concrete commitment of the heart reeks of hypocrisy, pretense and fraud. Mere words mean nothing. Christ suggested that our forgiving of others must be a complete purging of our heart *and* mind; a purifying of feeling and thought. To his followers, he proclaimed: *"Love your enemies, bless them that curse*

---

[140] Ephesians 1:6, 7.
[141] 3 Nephi 13:14, 15.

you, do good to them that hate you, and pray for them which despitefully use you." [142]

This sincere forgiveness of others, even our enemies, demands forgetfulness as well. Henry Ward Beecher offers this insightful expression: *"I can forgive but I cannot forget is another way of saying I cannot forgive."* [143]

In the Book of Mormon, Alma emphasizes that the people of God should be *"willing to bear one another's burdens, that they may be light."* [144] There is no question that sin is the heaviest burden of all. To have felt the Spirit of the Lord and then to have lost it by sin and become subject to the torturing and buffeting of the devil is the darkest, deepest tragedy of our human experience. Reach out with love, acceptance and honest forgiveness to all those who wander and stand in darkness. The miracle of forgiveness is available to all who turn from their unrighteous acts.

---

[142] Matthew 5:44.

[143] Source Unknown.

[144] Mosiah 18:8.

Ultimately there can be no success in sin. *"There are no successful sinners,"* wrote President Harold B. Lee. *"All must one day stand before God and be judged, each according to the deeds done in the flesh."* [145] Today is the day we must repent and put our lives in order. Our tomorrows are not guaranteed. We can do nothing about our past except repent. Today is the time for us to seek forgiveness. If we trust in the Lord and forgive others, then we, too, can be *"filled with joy, having received a remission of [our] sins, and having peace of conscience."* [146]

Elder John H. Groberg explained that partaking of the sacrament offers us the opportunity to experience the *"sweet, clean feeling of a pure soul having been forgiven and washed clean through the merits of the Savior."* Each Sunday we are given another occasion to think of the Savior, to have our sins forgiven and to have his Spirit guide us and comfort us. If all of us repented, determined decidedly to do better and then partook of the sacrament worthily, Elder Groberg informs, *"Oh, the life that would be given, the*

---

[145] Lee, Harold B., *Decisions for Successful Living,* Deseret Book Company, 1973. pp. 221, 222.
[146] Mosiah 4:3.

forgiveness that would be obtained, the spiritual strength that would be received.

"The light thus generated would cause Zion to shine forth brilliantly and would prepare a people pure in heart to be ready for the Lord's Second Coming." [147]

Whenever we become disheartened by our sinful nature, we must remember that Christ is eager for us to repent and receive his full mercy and forgiveness.

---

[147] Groberg, John H., *LDS Church News*, 1989.

Promise 10

Spiritually Begotten

"And now, because of the covenant which ye have made ye shall be called the children of Christ, his sons, and his daughters; for behold, this day he hath spiritually begotten you; for ye say that your hearts are changed through faith on his name; therefore, ye are born of him and have become his sons and his daughters." [148]

Although Jesus Christ holds the exclusive title of the *"Only Begotten Son"* of God the Father, [149] each one of

---

[148] Mosiah 5:7.
[149] 1 John 4:9; D&C 20:21.

us lived in a previous existence where we were spiritually begotten of Divine Parentage. In a very literal sense, all of us born on this earth are spiritually *"begotten sons and daughters unto God."* [150] However, in an additional sense, the Book of Mormon affirms that we can become *"spiritually begotten"* of Jesus Christ through our covenant to follow his teachings and obey his gospel. Just as we experienced a natural birth, we can also experience a spiritual birth and *"be called the children of Christ."* [151]

Our natural birth required that we leave our heavenly home, where we dwelt as spirits in divine companionship of our heavenly Parents, to begin a new, mortal life on earth. This physical birth created a fallen state in which we became, by nature, carnal, sensual and devilish. Our earth life is acutely governed by physical desires, appetites and passions and we are aware and susceptible to everything that is evil and wicked in this world. In this state, the natural man has become an enemy to God.

When we are spiritually begotten, or born of Christ, we begin a new life of righteousness and we become the sons and daughters of Jesus Christ. We

---

[150] Hebrews 12:9; D&C 76:24.
[151] Moroni 5:7.

call ourselves Christians as we take upon us the name of Christ and we become joint-heirs with him in the fullness of the glory of the Father. This spiritual re-birth changes our temperament and nature and initiates within us an enriched existence of spirituality and righteousness with tempered passions and disciplined desires.

Elder James E. Talmage explained that: *"By the new birth—that of water and the Spirit—mankind may become children of Jesus Christ, being through the means by Him provided 'begotten sons and daughters unto God'.* [152] *This solemn truth is further emphasized in the words of the Lord Jesus Christ given through Joseph Smith in 1833: 'And now, verily I say unto you, I was in the beginning with the Father, and am the Firstborn; And all those who are begotten through me are partakers of the glory of the same, and are the church of the Firstborn.'"* [153] [154]

The Doctrine and Covenants instructs us to take upon ourselves the name of Christ affirming that *"Jesus Christ is the name which is given of the Father, and there is none other name given whereby man can be saved; wherefore, all men must take upon them the*

---

[152] D&C 76:24.

[153] D&C 93:21, 22.

[154] Talmage, James E. *The Articles of Faith,* 1924, p. 470.

name which is given of the Father, for in that name shall they be called at the last day; wherefore, if they know not the name by which they are called, they cannot have place in the kingdom of my Father." [155]

Scripturally speaking, we must crucify *"the old man of sin"* and personify a *"new creation"* of the Holy Ghost. [156] When we are spiritually begotten, we no longer continue in our sinful ways [157] because we have *"no more disposition to do evil, but to do good continually."* [158]

Of course, we are not automatically born to a newness of life simply through our acceptance of the gospel, but our belief and acceptance of the Savior gives us the power to become spiritually begotten of Christ. As Bruce R. McConkie explains: *"It goes step by step, degree by degree, level by level, from a lower state to a higher, from grace to grace, until the time that the individual is wholly turned to the cause of righteousness. Now this means that an individual overcomes one sin today and another sin tomorrow. He perfects his life in one field now, and in another field*

---

[155] D&C 18:21-25.

[156] See Romans 6:6; 2 Corinthians 5:17.

[157] 1 John 3:8 JST.

[158] Mosiah 5:2.

later on. And the conversion process goes on, until it is completed, until we become, literally, as the Book of Mormon says, saints of God instead of natural men." 159

When we receive Christ and believe in our hearts that he is the Son of God; when we subsequently covenant in the waters of baptism to obey and to serve him; we take upon ourselves his name and are then given the power to become his sons and daughters.

---

159 McConkie, Bruce R., From an address given at BYU First Stake Conference, 11 February 1968.

Promise 11

Put on Immortality

"Even this mortal shall put on immortality, and this corruption shall put on incorruption, and shall be brought to stand before the bar of God, to be judged of him according to their works whether they be good or whether they be evil." [160]

The concept of immortality is one of the most extensive and enduring ideas in history. The possibility of life beyond the grave so intimately impacts all human hope and happiness that expert or amateur, prosperous or poor, academic or uneducated, religious or rebellious have all reflected on the immortality of the soul.

---

[160] Mosiah 6:10.

The Lord revealed to the prophet Moses that: *"This is my work and my glory; to bring to pass the immortality and eternal life of man."* [161] Since the commencement of time, the doctrine of immortality has encompassed all of civilization. The great foundational stone of every religion is intermingled with the notion of an eternal relationship with Deity and an existence beyond death and the grave. A belief in a future existence is the fundamental hope in virtually every religion in history.

The prevalent religions of the ancient world assured their participants a joyful and glorified continuation of life beyond the grave. The ancient religions of India, China, Egypt, Persia, Mesopotamia, Greece and Rome all maintained a belief in the immortality of man.

Over 5,000 years ago, the Sumerian society included many items and articles in their tombs which they thought would be useful to the dead in their journey through immortality. A principal precept of the ancient Mesopotamian empire was immortality of the soul. 3,000 years before Christ, the Egyptians embalmed their deceased in expectation of a literal revivification of the body. The Egyptian deity, Osiris,

---

[161] Moses 1:39.

identified as the god of the after-life, assured his faithful followers resurrection and rewards for righteousness.

Attributed to Confucius about 600 years before Christ is the statement: *"Man never dies. It is because men see only their bodies that they hate death."* [162] Chinese philosopher, Lao-Tzu, a contemporary of Confucius, taught that *"the wise man provides for the soul and not for the senses.... Being of Tao he endures forever; for though the body perish, yet he suffers no hurt."* [163] The Hindu bible instructs: *"There is an immortal portion of thee. Transport it to the world of the holy."* [164] Both Buddhist and Persian writings endorse immortality and the concept of heaven and hell as explicitly as does Christian theology. The ancient Greek philosophers also believed life was immortal and that *"they do not die, but that the dead go to join their god."* [165] Socrates is purported to have said, *"When death attacks a man, his immortal part retreats before death, and goes away safe and indestructible."* [166]

---

[162] Woodward, Hugh M., *Humanity's Greatest Need*, p. 294.

[163] *Ibid.*, p. 293.

[164] *Ibid.*, p. 292.

[165] Herodotus, vol. 4, p. 93.

[166] Bennion, Lynn M., *The Challenge of Immortality,* Week-Day Religious Education.

Even the world's prominent scientists believed in the concept of immortality. Charles Darwin expressed his own belief in immortality: *"Believing as I do that man in the distant future will be a far more perfect creature than he now is, it is an intolerable thought that he and all other sentient beings are doomed to complete annihilation after such long-continued slow progress. To those who fully admit the immortality of the human soul, the destruction of our world will not appear so dreadful."* [167]

Dr. Arthur H. Compton, the American physicist who won the Nobel Prize in Physics in 1927, claimed that: *"No cogent reason remains for supposing the soul dies with the body.... We (scientists) found strong reasons for believing that man is of extraordinary importance in the cosmic scheme.... What shall Nature do with him, annihilate him? What infinite waste! As long as there is in heaven a God of love there must be for God's children everlasting life!"* [168]

The Old Testament includes only brief indications of the doctrine of immortality. One of the most clear-cut statements regarding immortality from

---

[167] Darwin, Charles, *John Bartlett's Familiar Quotations*, p. 449.
[168] Source Unknown.

Daniel maintains that: *"Many of them that slept in the dust of the earth shall awake, some to everlasting life, and some to shame and everlasting contempt."* [169]

Isaiah is equally as clear: *"Thy dead men shall live, together with my dead body shall they arise. Awake and sing ye that dwell in dust: for thy dew is as the dew of herbs, and the earth shall cast out the dead."* [170]

The prophet who recorded the experiences of Job declared: *"For I know that my Redeemer liveth, and that he shall stand at the latter days upon the earth: and though after my skin worms destroy this body, yet in my flesh I shall see God."* [171]

Ecclesiastes gives us this consoling thought: *"Then shall the dust return to the earth as it was: and the spirit shall return unto God who gave it."* [172]

The New Testament is replete with evidence of both a pre-mortal and post-mortal existence. Jesus told his apostles, *"In my Father's house are many*

---

[169] Daniel 12:2.
[170] Isaiah 26:19.
[171] Job 19:25, 26.
[172] Ecclesiastes 12:7.

mansions; if it were not so I would have told you. I go to prepare a place for you." [173]

Paul distinctly describes this doctrine in his epistle written to the Corinthian saints:

"But now is Christ risen from the dead, and become the firstfruits of them that slept... For as in Adam all die, even so in Christ shall all be made alive... and this mortal must put on immortality." [174]

The doctrine and concept of immortality as recorded in the Book of Mormon is similarly distinct, dynamic, and detailed. The religion of ancient America advocated an acute belief in the eternal nature of human existence. They viewed mortal life as nothing more than a probationary state in preparation for a greater and more glorious existence beyond the grave. [175] The Nephite prophets of the Book of Mormon conveyed a broader, more extensive interpretation of immortality than any other ancient writings, religions or philosophies.

To the ancient Nephites, immortality implicated not only the preservation of personality, but included

---

[173] John 14:2.
[174] 1 Corinthians 15: 20, 22, 53.
[175] See 2 Nephi 2:19-29.

the permanent reuniting of the spirit with the body. As Amulek emphatically indicated:

"I say unto you that this mortal body is raised to an immortal body, that is from death, even from the first death unto life, that they can die no more; their spirits uniting with their bodies, never to be divided; thus the whole becoming spiritual and immortal, that they can no more see corruption." [176]

Finally, the prophet Abinadi identified the impossibility of immortality without the intercession of a savior: *"And if Christ had not risen from the dead, or have broken the bands of death that the grave should have no victory, and that death should have no sting, there could have been no resurrection, but there is a resurrection, therefore.... Even this mortal shall put on immortality, and this corruption shall put on incorruption, and shall be brought to stand before the bar of God."* [177]

The promise of immortality, as explained in the Book of Mormon, is extended to and embraces every living creature through Christ's resurrection. Abinadi assures us that death shall be destroyed and immortality shall gain its victory. Furthermore, the

---

[176] Alma 11:45.
[177] Mosiah 16:7-10.

apostle Paul taught us that: *"As in Adam all die, even so in Christ shall all be made alive, but every man in his own order; Christ the first fruits; afterwards they that are Christ's at his coming.... For he must reign till he hath put all enemies under his feet. The last enemy that shall be destroyed is death."* [178]

If even one solitary soul remains unredeemed from an earthly grave, then death has not been undone. Every person, regardless of who they are or how they have lived, must be resurrected. The promise of resurrection is as extensive as was the curse that first introduced death into our world.

Brent A. Barlow beautifully stated that *"The belief that the road of life merges into an endless freeway that leads to a more beautiful home and more fruitful life than any experience in mortality has been the inspiration of the great souls in all ages. This belief, older than the pyramids, antedating the first record of man's thoughts, has been firmly established in the minds and consciousness of the human race. There is a remarkable unanimity on this subject among the leaders throughout the ages, regardless of their adherence to other aspects of religion. This almost universal belief inspires hope, faith, and fortitude as we*

---

[178] 1 Corinthians 15:22-26.

approach our turn to join that innumerable caravan and take our place in the sacred halls of death." [179]

To the faithful, immortality becomes simply a means to an end—that end being our eternal salvation. The word of God reveals to us the magnificence and splendor of the glorious afterlife realized by the righteous. In the words revealed to the prophet Joseph Smith, the Lord has declared: *"For man is spirit. The elements are eternal, and spirit and element, inseparably connected, receive a fulness of joy; And when separated, man cannot receive a fulness of joy."* [180]

"We are," according to Neal A. Maxwell, *"immortal individuals whose constant challenge is to apply immortal principles to life's constantly changing situations."* [181]

---

[179] Barlow, Brent A., *Understanding Death,* Deseret Book Company, 1979.
[180] D&C 93:33, 34.
[181] *LDS Church News*, 1998.

Promise 12

Redeemed from Sin

"And remember also the words which Amulek spake unto Zeezrom, in the city of Ammonihah; for he said unto him that the Lord surely should come to redeem his people, but that he should not come to redeem them in their sins, but to redeem them from their sins.

"And he hath power given unto him from the Father to redeem them from their sins because of repentance; therefore he hath sent his angels to declare the tidings of the conditions of repentance, which bringeth unto the power of the Redeemer, unto the salvation of their souls." [182]

---

[182] Helaman 5:10, 11.

All humanity is redeemed from physical death because of the death and resurrection of our Savior, Jesus Christ. Every person who has ever lived on this earth will conquer death, defeat the grave and ascend into immortality. But overcoming physical death by itself is insufficient. Adam's fall affected changes not just in us but in the earth itself and all life on it. Malachi reveals that we have neither root nor branch. [183]

We are spiritual orphans; children without spiritual parents in this world. We need to be deemed worthy (re-deemed) of again being called the sons and daughters of God. Our spiritual death is a separation between us and God. Without the Savior's atonement, or in other words, without suitable reconciliation, we lose our divine relationship with God and forfeit our eternal life with him.

Christ's infinite atonement overcame our mortal death but in addition to that, it also redeemed us from our spiritual death. As Elder Bruce R. McConkie so articulately and persuasively illustrates: *"Our Lord's atoning sacrifice was one in which he conquered both temporal and spiritual death.... All men come forth from the grave in immortality; all are resurrected. Adam's fall enables body and spirit to separate in the*

---

[183] Malachi 4:1.

natural death; Christ's atonement causes body and spirit to reunite, inseparably, in immortality, never again to see that corruption which returns a mortal body to the dust whence its elements came. 'O grave, where is thy victory?' [184] *Truly, it is swallowed up by Him who holds the keys of death.*

"But immortality alone does not suffice.... The full glory of the atoning sacrifice of the Holy Messiah causes man to return to the presence of his God and to enjoy that kind and quality and state of life which is the possession of him who is the Father of us all. Those who, through faith and repentance and righteousness, are redeemed from the spiritual fall are raised not alone in immortality but unto eternal life.... They are reconciled to God spiritually. They are redeemed in the full sense of the word." [185]

God does not delight in punishing his children. Lehi taught that Adam fell so that men might be and that men are that they might have joy. [186] God's plan and purpose was never to denounce, destroy or

---

[184] 1 Corinthians 15:55.

[185] McConkie, Bruce R., *The Promised Messiah: The First Coming of Christ,* Deseret Book Company, 1978.

[186] 2 Nephi 2:25.

demolish the human race. His singular intent and interest are in saving everyone who pursues and pleads for salvation. The Lord assured Moses that his work and his glory is *"to bring to pass the immortality and eternal life of man."* [187] We have our agency and with it we can choose God's blessings or God's punishment. But we have also been given a way out.

Redemption from sin and a restoration to righteousness through the blessings of the atonement require we exercise faith in Jesus Christ and repent of our wrong choices. When we *"bow down before God, and call on his name in faith,"* [188] the hope of an eternal life can again be ours.

As Richard L. Evans explains: *"Repentance is part of the process of progress, of learning, of maturing, of recognizing law, of recognizing results; it is a process of facing facts. Every correcting of a mistake is a kind of repentance; every sincere apology is a kind of repentance; every improvement is a kind of repentance; every conquering of an unhealthful habit."* [189]

---

[187] Moses 1:39.

[188] Alma 22:15-18.

[189] Evans, Richard L., *Repentance-A Foremost Principle,* Improvement Era, January 1965.

The Book of Mormon clearly states that salvation is *"through the atonement which was prepared from the foundation of the world for all mankind, which ever were since the fall of Adam, or who are, or who ever shall be even unto the end of the world. And this is the means whereby salvation cometh. And there is none other salvation save this which hath been spoken of."* [190]

Christ bore the effects of the sins of all of God's children. The Sinless One became the great sinner [191] and in Gethsemane and on Calvary shouldered the awful anguish, suffering and heartbreak of our burden of guilt. Our Savior and Redeemer *"descended in suffering below that which man can suffer; or, in other words, he suffered greater sufferings and was exposed to more powerful contradictions than any man can be."* [192] The One who merited the least suffering suffered the most when he descended below all things. [193] Consequently, Christ *"hath power given unto him from the Father to redeem them from their sins because of repentance."* [194]

---

[190] Mosiah 4:7, 8.

[191] See 2 Corinthians 5:21; Galatians 3:13; Hebrews 2:9.

[192] Smith, Joseph, *Lectures on Faith* 5:2.

[193] See 2 Corinthians 8:9; Ephesians 4:8-10; D&C 88:6.

[194] Helaman 5:11.

Boyd K. Packer explained: *"Before the crucifixion and afterward, many men have willingly given their lives in selfless acts of heroism. But none faced what the Christ endured. Upon Him was the burden of all human transgression, all human guilt.... How the Atonement was wrought we do not know. No mortal watched as evil turned away and hid in shame before the light of that pure being. All wickedness could not quench that light. When what was done was done, the ransom had been paid. Both death and hell forsook their claim on all who would repent. Men at last were free. Then every soul who ever lived could choose to touch that light and be redeemed."* [195]

Helaman illustrates by what power Christ carried out his divine mission and calling: *"And he hath power given unto him from the Father to redeem them from their sins because of repentance."* [196] Only Jesus could put into effect the great plan of mercy. He did what he did because of who he was. He was a sinless offering. His was a voluntary offering. He was the son of Elohim, the Almighty God, in the most literal sense and as such, he inherited the powers of life and immortality.

---

[195] Packer, Boyd K., *Let Not Your Heart Be Troubled,* p. 76.
[196] Helaman 5:11.

Jesus was born as a man but was more than man. He was born a human but with a mission that required a super-human endowment. Jesus was subject to the temptations and attractions of mortality and possessed the capacity to suffer and die. Because he had been empowered and endowed in this manner, Christ could do for us what we could not do for ourselves.

C. S. Lewis observed: *"I have heard some people complain that if Jesus was God as well as man, then His sufferings and death lose all value in their eyes, 'because it must have been so easy for him.' Others may (very rightly) rebuke the ingratitude and ungraciousness of this objection; what staggers me is the misunderstanding it betrays. In one sense, of course, those who make it are right. They have even understated their own case. The perfect submission, the perfect suffering, the perfect death were... possible only because He was God. But surely that is a very odd reason for not accepting them... If I am drowning in a rapid river, a man who still has one foot on the bank may give me a hand which saves my life. Ought I to shout back (between my gasps) 'No, it's not fair! You have an advantage! You're keeping one foot on the bank'? That advantage—call it 'unfair' if you like—is the only reason why he can be of any use to me. To what will you look for help if you will not look to that which is stronger than yourself?"* [197]

We are redeemed from sin as the Lord takes our sins upon himself and imputes his righteousness to us. Helaman explains this concept to us:

"It is upon the rock of our Redeemer, who is Christ, the Son of God, that ye must build your foundation; that when the devil shall send forth his mighty winds, yea, his shafts in the whirlwind, yea, when all his hail and his mighty storm shall beat upon you, it shall have no power over you to drag you down to the gulf of misery and endless wo, because of the rock upon which ye are built, which is a sure foundation, a foundation whereon if men build they cannot fall." [198]

Because of our Redeemer, Jesus Christ, there is no obstacle to eternal life too great to overcome. Because of him, our minds may be at peace, our souls may rest. In the words of Paul: *"Be ye reconciled to God."* [199]

---

[197] Lewis, C. S., *Mere Christianity,* Collins, London, 1988.
[198] Helaman 5:12.
[199] 2 Corinthians 5:20.

Promise 13

Sanctified in Christ

"And again, if ye by the grace of God are perfect in Christ, and deny not his power, then are ye sanctified in Christ by the grace of God, through the shedding of the blood of Christ, which is in the covenant of the Father unto the remission of your sins, that ye become holy, without spot." [200]

Sanctify means to purify or to free from sin. Being sanctified means to be clean, pure, and spotless; to be free from the sins of this world; to become a new creature of the Holy Ghost renewed by the rebirth of the Spirit. Sanctification is a state of purity, holiness, and

---

[200] Moroni 10:33.

saintliness that comes through the cleansing power of the Holy Ghost. It is a state attained only by obedience to the laws and ordinances of the gospel. Ultimately, sanctification is a personal reward for personal righteousness.

But what, in all practicality, does sanctification mean and is it actually possible to attain sanctification in mortality?

Sanctification is one of the basic doctrines of the gospel of Christ. [201] We obtain sanctification only through keeping the principles and ordinances of the gospel. In the Book of Mormon, we are told to believe, repent, and be baptized so that we *"may be sanctified by the reception of the Holy Ghost, that ye may stand spotless before me at the last day. Verily, verily, I say unto you, this is my gospel."* [202] The Lord's plan of salvation is the method and the means which allow us to sanctify our souls and be made worthy of our heavenly inheritance.

Moroni portrays the plan of salvation in his counsel for us to *"come unto Christ, and be perfected in him, and deny yourselves of all ungodliness; and if*

---

[201] See D&C 20:31-34.
[202] 3 Nephi 27:20, 21.

ye shall deny yourselves of all ungodliness, and love God with all your might, mind and strength, then is his grace sufficient for you, that by his grace ye may be perfect in Christ; and if by the grace of God ye are perfect in Christ, ye can in nowise deny the power of God.

"And again, if ye by the grace of God are perfect in Christ, and deny not his power, then are ye sanctified in Christ by the grace of God, through the shedding of the blood of Christ, which is in the covenant of the Father unto the remission of your sins, that ye become holy, without spot." [203]

Sanctification, as we understand it, is not a singular event but a life-long process of gradual progression, improvement and refinement. It is the process by which we become holy. We may become sanctified as a manifestation of the Savior's mercy toward us: "And we know also, that sanctification through the grace of our Lord and Savior Jesus Christ is just and true, to all those who love and serve God with all their mights, minds, and strength." [204]

---

[203] Moroni 10:32, 33.
[204] D&C 20:31.

When we willingly concede our agency to God, we begin the procedure for eventually expelling and ousting the natural tendencies of mortality from our souls. This unswerving submission to the mind of God strengthens faith, enlarges humility, and instills a quality of Christ-like meekness in us. This experience gives us a newness of heart, creating the requisite conditions for sanctification. All of this is made possible through the atonement of Jesus Christ.

Brigham Young taught: *"I will put my own definition to the term sanctification, and say it consists in overcoming every sin and bringing all into subjection to the law of Christ. God has placed in us a pure spirit; when this reigns predominant, without let or hindrance, and triumphs over the flesh and rules and governs and controls as the Lord controls the heavens and the earth, this I call the blessing of sanctification. Will sin be perfectly destroyed? No, it will not, for it is not so designed in the economy of heaven.*

"Do not suppose that we shall ever in the flesh be free from temptations to sin. Some suppose that they can in the flesh be sanctified body and spirit and become so pure that they will never again feel the effects of the power of the adversary of truth. Were it possible for a person to attain to this degree of perfection in the flesh, he could not die, neither remain

in a world where sin predominates. Sin has entered into the world, and death by sin. [205] *I think we shall more or less feel the effects of sin so long as we live, and finally have to pass the ordeals of death.... We should so live as to make the world and all its natural blessings subservient to our reasonable wants and holy desires.*" [206]

The Book of Mormon explains that our mortal probation is a time to prepare to meet God. We are faced with a seemingly endless succession of circumstances forcing us to choose and decide. We face new challenges daily in our faith, our families, our friendships, and our professions. Making correct decisions and appropriate choices, for both our temporal and spiritual benefit, will greatly impact our sanctification.

The process for sanctification is described by King Benjamin in the Book of Mormon:

"*For the natural man is an enemy to God, and has been from the fall of Adam, and will be, forever and ever, unless he yields to the enticings of the Holy Spirit, and putteth off the natural man and becometh a saint through the atonement of Christ the Lord, and*

---

[205] Romans 5:12.

[206] Young, Brigham. *Journal of Discourses* 10:173.

becometh as a child, submissive, meek, humble, patient, full of love, willing to submit to all things which the Lord seeth fit to inflict upon him, even as a child doth submit to his father." [207]

The Holy Ghost is the sanctifier. Our hearts must become cleansed through the purification process to allow the Holy Ghost to abide with us and to permit its influence to dwell in us. By subordinating our will to the mind and will of God, our hearts can become purified and sanctified.

Our personal sanctification is possible only through the atonement of Jesus Christ. Endlessly falling short of the unbearable burden of perfectionism portrayed in the Savior's directive to *"be perfect even as I, or your Father who is in heaven is perfect,"* [208] emphasizes our complete and unconditional dependence on Jesus Christ. Despite our natural faults, failings and deficiencies, because of our hope in Christ we can maintain a presence of peace and optimism as we progress toward sanctification.

While defeating the temptations and attractions of this world in order to meet the criteria for

---

[207] Mosiah 3:19.
[208] 3 Nephi 12:48.

sanctification may seem nearly impossible, Mormon offers us a realistic approach to conquering these natural faults, failings and deficiencies:

"Nevertheless they did fast and pray oft, and did wax stronger and stronger in their humility, and firmer and firmer in the faith of Christ, unto the filling their souls with joy and consolation, yea, even to the purifying and the sanctification of their hearts, which sanctification cometh because of their yielding their hearts unto God." [209]

Sanctification is a process, not an event. Through the development of prayer and fasting we can obtain greater humility and firmer faith. In Mormon's portrayal of sanctification, the word "wax" suggests: *"to increase in extent, quantity, intensity, power, etc."* [210] We can fast and pray to increase the extent, quantity, intensity and power of our faith and humility.

Sanctification is a requirement to enter the kingdom of heaven. As we abide in the truth and become sanctified in this life, we will ultimately attain

---

[209] Helaman 3:35.

[210] An online dictionary definition.

an inheritance with the sanctified in the celestial kingdom.

"And unto him that repenteth and sanctifieth himself before the Lord shall be given eternal life." [211]

As we demonstrate a commitment to Christ, surrendering our hearts to God and cleansing ourselves from all unrighteousness, we can become sanctified through the atonement and grace of Jesus Christ. [212] Being sanctified, however, is not an unconditional assurance of salvation. This warning comes from the Lord: *"There is a possibility that man may fall from grace and depart from the living God; Therefore let the church take heed and pray always, lest they fall into temptation; Yea, and even let those who are sanctified take heed also."* [213]

Through righteous living and with the purifying power of the Holy Ghost, we can yield to the mind and will of God voluntarily and without compulsion. Ousting the carnal content from our hearts is the spiritualization of our terrestrial state. Faithfully giving ourselves to God requires that we confront our corporal

---

[211] D&C 133:62.

[212] 2 Nephi 31:19, 20.

[213] D&C 20:32-34.

nature and declare spiritual war against the destructive characteristics of immorality.

We discover the means and methods of attaining sanctification through a lifetime of choices and decisions congruent with the will of God. In the Book of Mormon, the prophet Alma describes the conditions of those who had achieved the status of sanctification:

"They were called after this holy order, and were sanctified, and their garments were washed white through the blood of the Lamb. Now they, after being sanctified by the Holy Ghost, having their garments made white, being pure and spotless before God, could not look upon sin save it were with abhorrence; and there were many, exceeding great many, who were made pure and entered into the rest of the Lord their God." [214]

The secret to attaining sanctification is in purifying our purposes, our intentions and our desires by surrendering our hearts to God. By yielding our objectives to God's will, we emulate God and become spiritual creatures with God-like attributes. This cannot be a fractional or partial effort on our parts. Sanctification of our souls requires a comprehensive

---

[214] Alma 13:11, 12.

and unconditional surrender of our wills to God. C. S. Lewis clarifies this commitment as follows:

"Christ says, 'Give me All. I don't want so much of your time and so much of your money and so much of your work: I want You. I have not come to torment your natural self, but to kill it. No half-measures are any good. I don't want to cut off a branch here and a branch there. I want to have the whole tree down. I don't want to drill the tooth, or crown it, or stop it, but to have it out. Hand over the whole natural self, all the desires which you think innocent as well as the ones you think wicked—the whole outfit. I will give you a new self instead. In fact, I will give you Myself: My own will shall become yours.'" [215]

---

[215] Lewis, C. S., *Mere Christianity*, 1952. New York: Macmillan, 1960.

Promise 14

The Gate of Heaven is Open

"Yea, thus we see that the gate of heaven is open unto all, even to those who will believe on the name of Jesus Christ, who is the Son of God." [216]

Aaron, a Nephite prince who forsook the throne to preach the word of God, asked this question of the Amalekites: *"Believest thou that the Son of God shall come to redeem mankind from their sins?"* He then testified to them that *"there could be no redemption for*

---

[216] Helaman 3:28.

mankind save it were through the death and sufferings of Christ, and the atonement of his blood." [217]

Amulek began a discourse to the Zoramites with the question of *"whether the word be in the Son of God, or whether there shall be no Christ."* He answered that question with his testimony that *"the word is in Christ unto salvation."* [218]

Written *"by the spirit of prophecy and of revelation,"* the purpose of the Book of Mormon is to convince *"the Jew and Gentile that Jesus is the Christ, the Eternal God"* [219] and that *"the gate of heaven is open unto all, even to those who will believe on the name of Jesus Christ, who is the Son of God."* [220]

Our purpose in this life, the objective of mortality, is to have joy, peace and contentment and to gain eternal life in the hereafter. *"The greatest gift that a person can have in eternity,"* Elder Bruce R. McConkie taught, *"is to have eternal life, which is to go*

---

[217] Alma 21:7,9.

[218] Alma 34:5,6.

[219] Title Page, *Book of Mormon*.

[220] Helaman 3:28.

where God is and have the kind of existence and kind of life that he has." [221]

Elder McConkie tells us that *"if you wanted to draw a picture of the plan of salvation, you could draw a gate and then write by the side of that gate the name, 'Repentance and Baptism.' Then, from the gate a long, long distance upward you could draw a path, a narrow course, and you could write the name, 'The Strait and Narrow Path,' by this path. And then at the end of the path you could write the words, 'The Kingdom of God,' or 'Eternal Life.'"* [222]

The Book of Mormon teaches us that *"the gate by which ye should enter is repentance and baptism by water; and then cometh a remission of your sins by fire and by the Holy Ghost.*

"And then are ye in this strait and narrow path which leads to eternal life; yea, ye have entered in by the gate; ye have done according to the

---

[221] McConkie, Bruce R., *Sermons and Writings of Bruce R. McConkie*, Deseret Book Company, 1989
[222] Ibid.

commentary *commandments of the Father and the Son; and ye have received the Holy Ghost."* [223]

We act on the gospel message to the extent that we believe in Christ. Only through faith and a knowledge of Christ can we enter at the gate. This we do by accepting the gospel and receiving the Holy Ghost. We are reminded in the Book of Mormon that *"ye have not come thus far save it were by the word of Christ with unshaken faith in him, relying wholly upon the merits of him who is mighty to save."* [224] In other words, we can be saved and obtain an inheritance in the kingdom of God only when we have acquired faith in Jesus Christ.

As we develop faith, we must repent of our sins. We must be washed clean in the waters of baptism. Then we may receive the gift of the Holy Ghost, the right to the constant companionship of that member of the Godhead. We are given the privilege and right to have the Holy Ghost speak to our spirit and declare truth to us with such conviction and certainty that it cannot be contested. Nephi tells us that *"angels speak by the power of the Holy Ghost; wherefore, they speak the*

---

[223] 2 Nephi 31:17,18.
[224] 2 Nephi 31:19.

words of Christ," and that "the words of Christ will tell you all things what ye should do." [225] It is by this great gift of the Holy Ghost that we will have power to sanctify ourselves and do what is needed for our salvation.

Entering at the gate of repentance and baptism, we can have our sins washed clean in the blood of Christ through his atoning sacrifice. As we move forward and hold fast to that which is good, we proceed along the strait and narrow path toward eternal life and an inheritance in the celestial kingdom.

Once we have entered at the gate, we "must press forward with a steadfastness in Christ... feasting upon the word of Christ, and endure to the end" [226] for "unless a man shall endure to the end, in following the example of the Son of the living God, he cannot be saved." [227]

The first fruits of faith are repentance and baptism. We abandon our carnal nature and covenant with God to keep his commandments and always remember the name of Christ. The Book of Mormon reveals that if we will repent of our sins and covenant

---

[225] 2 Nephi 32:3.
[226] 2 Nephi 31:20.
[227] 2 Nephi 31:16.

to obey our Father in Heaven, and be baptized by water, we will then receive the baptism of fire and the Holy Ghost, which will bring a mighty change to our hearts, even as it did with Alma the elder.

"And according to his faith, there was a mighty change wrought in his heart.... And behold, he preached the word unto your fathers, and a mighty change was also wrought in their hearts." [228]

The entire gospel of Jesus Christ can be encapsulated in the distinctive dictum that *"whosoever putteth his trust in [Christ] the same shall be lifted up at the last day."* [229]

The way to come to Christ is through membership in his church. Many people question the need or reason for an organized church. Some believe they can accomplish their personal salvation without needing to attend church or fulfill other obligations. It is enough, they contend, to be honest and honorable and to do good. In reality, it is indispensable that we serve together in Christ's church and under the direction of his authorized servants to accomplish his purposes and to prove ourselves.

---

[228] Alma 5:12, 13.
[229] Mosiah 23:22.

We need the strength that comes from association with others who are seeking the same goals and we need to encourage and help one another because eventually we will all stand individually before Christ to account for our choices in life and to receive the rightful measure of justice and grace at his hand.

"O then, my beloved brethren, come unto the Lord, the Holy One. Remember that his paths are righteous. Behold, the way for man is narrow, but it lieth in a straight course before him, and the keeper of the gate is the Holy One of Israel; and he employeth no servant there; and there is none other way save it be by the gate; for he cannot be deceived, for the Lord God is his name." [230]

This reckoning is inevitable. We must all stand before the Keeper of the Gate prior to being permitted to enter the kingdom of Heaven. The hierarchy of earth will not be the hierarchy of heaven. The deprived and downhearted will be exalted and the prosperous and privileged will be disgraced. The infants and infirm will excel while the powerful and mighty will be humbled. Many will cry *"Lord! Lord!"* in that great upheaval of human expectations when *"many that are first shall be*

[230] 2 Nephi 9:41.

last; and the last shall be first." [231] Then we shall all understand just how reliant we are on the great atonement of our Lord and Redeemer.

---

[231] Matthew 19:30.

A Word About the Temple.

For us the temple is a gate of heaven.

Temples are among the holiest places on earth. In the temple we can come closest to God. We can better sense his presence and obtain his inspiration as we perform ordinances that reach beyond the veil and bless those who have passed on to another state of spiritual existence. All of us are saved on the same principles and ordinances of the gospel.

The sacred purpose for building temples is to perform in them the ordinances and endowments necessary so that all humanity may become heirs of God and joint-heirs with Jesus Christ and receive the fulness of the ordinances of his kingdom. Those who do not receive all the ordinances may come short of a fullness of glory. [232]

The temple is also a gate to heaven for those who died without receiving the sacred ordinances necessary for their salvation. At the dedication of the Los Angeles Temple, President Stephen L. Richards addressed how the power of the sealing ordinance reaches beyond our understanding.

---

[232] See *History of the Church* 5:423, 424.

He further quoted the prophet Joseph Smith, who stated that: *"The church is not fully organized, in its proper order, and cannot be, until the temple is completed, where places will be provided for the administration of the ordinances of the priesthood."* [233]

The temple is a stronghold of holiness in a wicked world. The influence imparted from the temple is more critically significant than we can comprehend.

---

[233] *History of the Church* 4:603.

Promise 15

Eternal Bliss

"For behold, it is as easy to give heed to the word of Christ, which will point to you a straight course to eternal bliss, as it was for our fathers to give heed to this compass, which would point unto them a straight course to the promised land." [234]

George Albert Smith stated very specifically that *"Happiness is what we are all seeking, and it is what our Father in heaven desires for us."* The nebulous notion of eternal bliss held by the majority of humanity; the fluffy clouds of heaven with its golden harps and

---

[234] Alma 37:44.

feather-winged angels beyond some pearly gate, is the professed goal-apparent of all religious endeavor.

One religious writer has depicted eternal bliss as *"seeing God face to face, unveiled as He really is. The 'face to face,' however, is literally true only of our blessed Saviour, who ascended into heaven with His sacred body. Otherwise, as God is a spirit, He has no body and consequently no face. In paradise, spirits (angels and our souls) see spirits. We shall see God and angels, not with the eye of the body, nor by the vibration of cosmic light, but with the spiritual eye, with the soul's intellectual perception, elevated by a supernatural influx from God.... the perfect image of God will be reflected on the soul, impressing on it a vivid representation of Him. We shall thus enjoy an intellectual possession of Him, very different from our possession of earthly things."*

Another prominent religious writer shares his distinct vision of eternal bliss as *"When I get to heaven, I shall spend the first five million years of my life in gazing upon the face of God; then if my wife is near I shall turn and look at her for five minutes. Then I shall gaze upon the glory of God again for a million million years; and when the longing of my eyes shall have been satisfied, and my soul is suffused with the beatific vision, I shall snatch up my harp and begin playing."*

The piercing light of revealed religion rapidly and completely evaporates these fabricated philosophies from the fields of eternal truth. The concept of eternal salvation consists of at least two underlying components that more accurately depict eternal realities; they are the anticipation of eternal life and the expectation of eternal bliss.

God has promised us extraordinary blessings as we learn to walk by faith and make morally good decisions and choices. His incredible plan providing us with the gift and miracle of eternal life in the presence of God and our Savior is a testament to how deeply he loves us and how much he desires our eternal happiness. His great plan of salvation includes our eternal bliss as well as our eternal life.

The secret to finding infinite happiness is found in obedience to the laws of the Great Plan of Happiness. John A. Widtsoe taught that *"the more completely law is obeyed, the greater the consciousness of perfect joy. Throughout eternal life, increasing intelligence is attained, leading to greater adaptation to law, resulting in increasingly greater joy. Therefore it is that eternal life is the greatest gift of God, and that the plan of salvation is priceless."* [235]

---

[235] Widtsoe, John A., *A Rational Theology*, p. 34.

Aristotle wrote that happiness is an *"activity of soul in accordance with virtue."* Happiness, in other words, is not a thing but an action or activity. We don't commonly refer to ourselves as 'faithful' members of the Church but instead as 'active' members. This is because faith, like happiness, is a principle of action.

Happiness, however, is not simply acting. It is acting *"in accordance with virtue."* Only virtuous activity creates happiness. When we seek to do good, when we strive to obey God's commandments, that is when we become candidates for happiness.

Joseph Smith clarifies for us that: *"Happiness is the object and design of our existence; and will be the end thereof, if we pursue the path that leads to it; and this path is virtue, uprightness, faithfulness, holiness, and keeping all the commandments of God.... In obedience there is joy and peace unspotted, unalloyed; and as God has designed our happiness—and the happiness of all his creatures, He never has—He never will institute an ordinance or give a commandment to His people that is not calculated in its nature to promote that happiness which He has designed, and which will not end in the greatest amount of good and glory to those who become the recipients of his law and ordinances."* [236]

The gospel of Jesus Christ is the Great Plan of Happiness. The only plan that will assure eternal bliss is the plan of eternal life advocated by our beloved Savior. Sorrow and disappointment are the inevitable results of disobeying the Father of our spirits and ignoring the gospel of Jesus Christ.

Rudger Clawson delivered the following message: *"If a man cannot enter the kingdom of God he cannot rise to a fulness of joy, never, worlds without end. He may get some joy, he may get great happiness from what he does do in righteousness, but to get a fulness he must be born again."* [237]

A fullness of joy and true happiness are never found in the frivolous or carnal pleasures of this world. Happiness comes only through God's infallible formula for eternal bliss.

George Q. Cannon explains that *"it is not given to men and women on the earth to be entirely satisfied,*

---

[236] Smith, Joseph, *Teachings of the Prophet Joseph Smith,* pp. 255-257.
[237] Clawson, Rudger, *Conference Report,* Oct 9-10, 1932.

if they seek for satisfaction and happiness in worldly things. There is only one way in which perfect happiness can be obtained, and that is by having the Spirit of God." [238]

The gospel of Jesus Christ is the code of conduct for obtaining happiness, joy and peace. As we live the teachings of the gospel, we will become engaged in assisting the Savior to bring about the eternal happiness of God's children. The duty of every member of the Church is to save souls, to do good and bless others. In other words, to act *"in accordance with virtue."*

President David O. McKay has declared: *"Pleasure is not the purpose of man's existence. Joy is."* [239] Happiness includes all that is really desirable and of true worth.

James E. Talmage differentiates between the deceptive pit of pleasure and the heights of true happiness. According to Brother Talmage, happiness is genuine gold; pleasure but gilded brass. Happiness is the genuine diamond; pleasure the paste imitation.

---

[238] Cannon, George Q., *Gospel Truth*, 2:317-18.
[239] McKay, David O., *Gospel Ideals*, p. 492.

Happiness is the ruby; pleasure is soft and brittle as stained glass.

Happiness requires no repentance or regret. It entails no remorse; pleasure often requires repentance, contrition, and suffering.

True happiness is lived over and over again in memory, always with a renewal of the original good; a moment of unholy pleasure may leave a barbed sting, which, like a thorn in the flesh, is an ever-present source of anguish.

Happiness springs from the deeper fountains of the soul. [240]

George Albert Smith taught that: *"Our mission in the world is to save souls, to bless them, and to place them in a condition that they may go back into the presence of our Father, crowned with glory, immortality and eternal life. Let kindness, joy and peace characterize our efforts, and be a blessing to our Father's children wherever it may be our privilege to roam. Let us extend to all our Father's children the hand of welcome.*

---

[240] See Talmage, James, *Improvement Era*, December 1913.

"All happiness that is worthy of the name is the result of keeping the commandments of our Heavenly Father—all happiness.

"If each day of our lives we do something to bless others, we will continue to accumulate peace, happiness, love, joy, satisfaction, and it will be a great joy to us when in the kingdom of our Heavenly Father we go on throughout the ages of eternity." [241]

Our service to others will assist them to reach that anticipated goal of everlasting life in the presence of our Heavenly Parents and Elder Brother and increase our infinite joy as well. [242] Our eternal bliss is a product of our service to others. This commission is three-fold in nature:

The first aspect of our service is to teach the gospel at home to family, friends and neighbors through our words as well as through our actions.

The second aspect of our service is to preach the word of God to the world's population.

---

[241] Smith, George Albert, *Improvement Era*, July 1945.
[242] See D&C 18:17.

The final aspect is to administer the saving gospel ordinances in temples for those who have passed on.

Through these three aspects of service to others, the blessings of the gospel will be brought to all of our Father's children, whether here or in the spirit world. This is the 'word of Christ' that points like a compass to the path of eternal bliss and happiness.

Promise 16

Filled with the Love of God

"And behold, I say unto you that if ye do this ye shall always rejoice, and be filled with the love of God, and always retain a remission of your sins; and ye shall grow in the knowledge of the glory of him that created you, or in the knowledge of that which is just and true." [243]

Just as pure water flows from a pure fountain, pure love pours from a pure heart. God's love for us creates our human capacity for pure and sincere love. True love originates with God and sheds *"itself abroad in the*

---

[243] Mosiah 4:12.

hearts of the children of men." [244] The apostle John revealed to us that *"God is love; and he that dwelleth in love dwelleth in God, and God in him."* [245] Eliminate God from the equation and we lose the capability to love fully and to love honestly. God is the genesis, the core and the source of all true love.

Our Father in heaven loves each one of us perfectly, completely, and unconditionally. His love for us is forever constant and eternally endless. Sometimes though, our ability to feel his love dissipates or fades. Christian author C. S. Lewis has written that *"the great thing to remember is that, though our feelings come and go, His love for us does not. It is not wearied by our sins, or our indifference."* [246]

God will always love us. Our capacity to sense his love, however, is reliant on our propensity toward obedience to his commandments. If we love the world, then the love of the Father is not in us. [247] Our perception of God's love, manifest through his Spirit, diminishes as our love of the world increases. God loves the sinner as well as the so-called saint but *"the*

---

[244] 1 Nephi 11:22.

[245] 1 John 4:16.

[246] Lewis, C. S., *Mere Christianity* Macmillan, 1952 pp. 102–3.

[247] See 1 John 2:15.

friendship of the world is enmity with God" and *"whosoever therefore will be a friend of the world is the enemy of God."* [248]

A fullness of love cannot exist without God. Simple mischievous missteps toward sin or even shameless indulgences in worldly desires do not decrease God's love for us but they absolutely will diminish the presence of his Spirit. [249] We may forfeit our ability to truly love through the loss of his Spirit. When we keep the commandments, we have his promise that his Spirit will be with us.

The prophet Joseph Smith taught that *"love is one of the chief characteristics of Deity, and ought to be manifested by those who aspire to be the sons of God."* [250] In the Book of Mormon, King Benjamin enumerates various approaches to becoming filled with the love of God. Remembering the greatness of God and our own nothingness are components of the

---

[248] James 4:4.

[249] See D&C 121:37.

[250] Smith, Joseph, *History of The Church of Jesus Christ of Latter-day Saints,* 4:227.

practice of God-like love. [251] John reminds us that we love God because he first loved us. [252]

God's love "is all-consuming and all-encompassing," explains President Ezra Taft Benson. "The breadth, depth, and height of this love of God extend into every facet of one's life. Our desires, be they spiritual or temporal, should be rooted in a love of the Lord." [253] As we begin to feel the affliction and liability of sin washed away in the blood of the Lamb, as the influence of his love lifts the load of remorse, shame and sorrow brought on through our weakness or our outright rebellion, we will begin to sense and understand the pure love of God toward us. When we conduct ourselves in ways that will permit the Spirit to dwell with us, our love for God will increase. As we begin to recognize his commitment, concern and contribution in our individual lives and acknowledge his hand in all things,[254] we will sense his love in even greater ways.

The restored gospel is a constant reminder of the principle of love. Alma advises us that we should

---

[251] See Mosiah 4:11, 12.

[252] See 1 John 4:10, 19.

[253] Benson, Ezra Taft, *Teachings of Ezra Taft Benson,* Bookcraft, 1988, p. 349.

[254] See D&C 59:21.

carry *"the love of God always in your hearts, that ye may be lifted up at the last day and enter into his rest."* [255] The Book of Mormon can be the channel to increase our understanding and improve our ability to feel and impart that love. It provides us with instruction on how we can become filled with love. It directs us in the proper methods and expressions of pure love and enlightens us on the aspects of charity, the pure love of Christ. We might ask ourselves: 'What can I personally do, beyond simply obeying the commandments, that will facilitate my ability to daily feel his love for me?'

We discover from the Book of Mormon that charity is *"the pure love of Christ"* and that it *"endureth forever."* [256] In other words, it is an *"everlasting love."* [257] The prophet Joseph Smith explains that *"the nearer we get to our Heavenly Father the more we are disposed to look with compassion on perishing souls; we feel that we want to take them upon our shoulders, and cast their sins behind our backs."* [258] To the extent

---

[255] Alma 13:29.

[256] Moroni 7:47.

[257] Moroni 8:17.

[258] Smith, Joseph, *Teachings of the Prophet Joseph Smith*, pp. 240-41.

that we *come unto Christ,* we *become as Christ* and can learn to love in the same divine manner that he loves.

The Christ-like characteristics of charity are outlined in the detailed description quoted by Moroni in the Book of Mormon: *"And charity suffereth long, and is kind, and envieth not, and is not puffed up, seeketh not her own, is not easily provoked, thinketh no evil, and rejoiceth not in iniquity but rejoiceth in the truth, beareth all things, believeth all things, hopeth all things, endureth all things. Wherefore, my beloved brethren, if ye have not charity, ye are nothing, for charity never faileth. Wherefore, cleave unto charity, which is the greatest of all, for all things must fail—but charity is the pure love of Christ, and it endureth forever; and whoso is found possessed of it at the last day, it shall be well with him."* [259]

As we exercise our faith and endeavor to become new creatures in Christ, we will find that the motives of our service to God and to others become selfless and sincere. When the source of our random acts of kindness, good deeds and service is charity, the pure love of Christ, our efforts are so much more effective and virtuous.

---

[259] Moroni 7:45-47.

Charity is a gift bestowed on us from God. It is a gift we are encouraged to seek and acquire. The spectrum of charity, the greatest of all the gifts of the Spirit, consists of nine components. Both Mormon and Paul [260] describe in their respective writings the essential components of a truly charitable person:

1. Patience   *Charity suffereth long.*
2. Kindness   *And is kind.*
3. Generosity *Charity envieth not.*
4. Humility   *Charity vaunteth not itself, is not puffed up.*
5. Courtesy   *Doth not behave itself unseemly.*
6. Unselfish   *Seeketh not her own.*
7. Good Temper *Is not easily provoked.*
8. Guileless   *Thinketh no evil.*
9. Sincere   *Rejoiceth not in iniquity but rejoiceth in the truth.*

Patience is the natural approach to love. Love is passive, calm, never in a hurry. A charitable person, blessed with a measure of the pure love of Christ, would also be given greater patience and a more loving perspective toward others and their particular circumstances.

---

[260] See Moroni 7:45-48 and 1 Corinthians 13:1-13.

Kindness is love in action. So much of Christ's life was spent in doing kind things. A charitable person is receptive to others' needs and is driven to do good and bless others.

True love is generous and never competitive. A charitable person is less interested in the achievements, accomplishments or accolades of others. Love seeks happiness in simple pleasures.

Humility, the fourth essential component of charity, turns the spotlight away from self and toward God. Humility is a seal on the lips and a forgetfulness in the mind when a service has been rendered. A charitable person recognizes the hand of God in all things and seeks his glory alone.

Courtesy is the societal side of love. A charitable person is polite to others regardless of their position, status or wealth. Courtesy is love in the little trivialities of day-to-day living.

Pure love is so unselfish in nature that it does not even seek that which rightfully belongs to it. One of the powerful lessons of Christ's life and teaching is that true happiness cannot be found in getting and having, only in serving and giving. There is no greatness in acquisitions. Greatness is found in unselfish love.

A charitable person displays meekness and poise under provocation. A bad temper may seem like a rather harmless weakness that simply comes and goes with the mood and circumstances of the day. And yet, Paul seemed impressed to include good tempered in his list of charitable qualities. A bad temperament may be considered the *"vice of the virtuous."* It is not a physical weakness but a weakness in our disposition. The prodigal son may have indulged in weaknesses of the flesh, but his older brother indulged in weaknesses of the heart and mind. Henry Drummond describes a bad temper as *"the occasional bubble escaping to the surface which betrays some rottenness underneath."* [261] A lack of the other essential charitable components is instantly revealed in one flash of bad temper.

True love is guileless and pure. It does not dwell on unrighteous thoughts or desires. A charitable person looks to encourage and strengthen others with no hidden agenda and no personal desires for glory. Pure love always has an eye single to the glory of God.

Pure love accepts only that which is true and real. A charitable person will search for the truth in all things. A heart filled with the love of God has no more

---

[261] Drummond, Henry, *The Greatest Thing in the World.* Collins Clear-Type Press, p. 37.

disposition to do evil but rather to do good continually.[262]

To this list of nine essential components, Moroni adds four more ingredients to developing a charitable nature:

A charitable person bears all things. Nothing is a hardship for love. A charitable person does not murmur or complain about the burdens of life with its continual cares, its malicious circumstances, its constant disappointments and displeasures, or with the small, sordid souls surrounding them. A charitable person does not resent the skilled potter's hand that is sculpting the still too shapeless character within. Christ tells us that his burden is light and that his yoke is easy.[263] When properly positioned, Christ's yoke is actually the easiest way of taking on life.

A charitable person believes all things. This means that the charitable person is open to truth through the gift of a believing heart.

A charitable person hopes all things. It is a hope founded in Christ; a vital, vibrant assurance that despite the struggles, weaknesses and temptations of

---

[262] See Mosiah 5:2.
[263] See Matthew 11:30.

life, eternal life in the realms of God and Christ is the end result of this earthly journey.

A charitable person endures all things. Every person on this beautiful planet passes through trials of one kind or another. We all have our personal crosses to bear. The true follower of Christ endures the tests, is shaped by the trials and is strengthened in the tribulations.

A Word About Ministering

The Book of Mormon affirms that service is essential to salvation. Love of God is vitally connected to love of others and the Book of Mormon provides a witness that when we are in the service of our fellow beings we are only in the service of our God. [264]

Service is absolutely essential if we desire to follow the Savior and become like him. President David O. McKay explains that *"If you want to love God, you have to learn to love and serve the people. That is the way to show your love for God."* [265] But service becomes valid and life-altering (for both us and for the person being served) only when it is influenced and encouraged by pure love.

Who we are and how well we love and serve God and his other children are so much more important and significant in the eternal aspect than what we actually do. The development of the greatest of all the gifts of God requires that we demonstrate greater concern for the needs of others over our own personal needs or

---

[264] See Mosiah 2:17.

[265] McKay, David O., *Stand Ye in Holy Places*, Deseret Book 1974, p. 189.

desires. As we begin to bear the burden of true Christian discipleship, we will recognize that service will have a lasting impact only when it is founded in the pure love of Christ.

We are counselled to pray for charity. We are advised to plead for it with all the energy of our hearts. As we do, charity will flow into our lives from our Savior, the fountain of pure love, and we will experience exalted and inspiring moments in which our hearts extend themselves to others with an affection previously unfelt or unnoticed. Eventually we will be persuaded, like the apostle Paul, *"that neither death, nor life, nor angels, nor principalities, nor powers, nor things present, nor things to come, nor height, nor depth, nor any other creature, shall be able to separate us from the love of God, which is in Christ Jesus our Lord."* [266]

The importance of developing the gift of charity cannot be overstated. Without charity we cannot be saved in the kingdom of God. [267] Without charity we

---

[266] Romans 8:38, 39.
[267] Moroni 10:21.

"cannot inherit that place... prepared in the mansions of thy Father." [268] Without Charity we are nothing. [269]

After his first vision, Joseph Smith tells us: "My soul was filled with love, and for many days I could rejoice with great joy, and the Lord was with me." [270] It is imperative to our salvation that we obtain the gift of charity. When the day comes that we dwell with our Savior, it will not be enough to merely be in his presence. When he comes we will want to be like him. We will want to be as righteous as he is, and we will long to love with that same pure gift with which he loves us—the spiritual gift of charity.

---

[268] Ether 12:34.

[269] Moroni 7:44.

[270] Backman Jr., Milton V., *Joseph Smith's First Vision,* Bookcraft, 1980, p. 157.

Promise 17

Written in the Book of Life

"For the names of the righteous shall be written in the book of life, and unto them will I grant an inheritance at my right hand. And now, my brethren, what have ye to say against this? I say unto you, if ye speak against it, it matters not, for the word of God must be fulfilled." [271]

No event in all eternity will ever match, in magnitude or meaning, the perfect atonement of our Savior, Jesus Christ. The redemption provided by the Redeemer and Rescuer of all humanity is of greater consequence and value than any incident that ever has or ever will occur in heaven or on earth. Joseph Smith taught that all

---

[271] Alma 5:58.

things *"which pertain to our religion are only appendages to it."* [272]

Christ's atoning sacrifice was the designed and determined channel of salvation for all humanity. It was the plan from the very beginning. Some believe the atonement was simply a backup plan, necessary only because of the choices Adam and Eve made in the garden. In reality, the plan for the entire human family has always been that redemption would come to *"worlds without number"* through Jesus Christ. [273]

When Adam asked the Lord, *"Why is it that men must repent and be baptized in water?"* the Lord told Adam:

"Behold I have forgiven thee thy transgression in the Garden of Eden." [274]

Even though the physical atonement would not take place for millennia, its universal influence, effect and validity were already assured. Adam's transgression was forgiven even though the atonement

---

[272] Smith, Joseph, *Teachings of the Prophet Joseph Smith,* Deseret Book, p. 121.
[273] Moses 1:33.
[274] Moses 6:53.

would not transpire until the great Jehovah became the mortal Jesus of Nazareth.

"And behold, Enoch saw the day of the coming of the Son of Man, even in the flesh; and his soul rejoiced, saying: The Righteous is lifted up, and the Lamb is slain from the foundation of the world; and through faith I am in the bosom of the Father, and behold, Zion is with me." [275]

Adam was forgiven when the majority of humanity, including the Sacrificial Lamb himself, still lived in a premortal life. Forgiveness was granted as if the sacred event had already occurred.

The saving influence of Christ's expiation is, and always has been, certain. Whether or not we accept it and act accordingly is the only uncertainty. Because of the atonement, the time will come when all of Father's children will stand before the Savior to be judged and that judgment will be based on the records kept on earth and in heaven.

John the Revelator saw two distinct records. One set of records he called *"books"*; and the other set

---

[275] Moses 7:47.

he referred to as *"the book of life."* [276] Everyone will be *"judged out of those things which were written in the books, according to their works."* [277]

What we do on earth is unquestionably catalogued in heaven. Our works of righteousness, our charity, our baptism, our temple marriage, our kindness toward others are all, according to scripture, known and written in the Lord's book of life. Everything is known and recorded by the discerning eye. Heaven is constantly auditing our earthly actions. All our doings are known to our Father in heaven.

The prophet Joseph Smith explained that: *"The dead were judged out of those things which were written in the books, according to their works; consequently, the books spoken of must be the books which contained the record of their works, and refer to the records which are kept on the earth. And the book which was the book of life is the record which is kept in heaven."* [278]

President Joseph Fielding Smith added this insight: *"Every man will be judged according to his*

---

[276] See Revelation 20:12.
[277] Revelation 20:12.
[278] D&C 128:7.

works, his opportunities for receiving the truth, and the intent of his heart." [279]

We will be judged by our works out of the things written in the books. What we do on earth is recorded in the books of both heaven and earth, and our works form the basis of our judgment. The ancient Nephite prophet Jacob wrote: *"When all men shall have passed from this first death unto life, insomuch as they have become immortal, they must appear before the judgment-seat of the Holy One of Israel; and then cometh the judgment, and then must they be judged according to the holy judgment of God."* [280] The apostle Paul later also testified that: *"Every one of us shall give account of himself to God."* [281]

A clarification of the meaning and function of the book of life was offered by Bruce R. McConkie: *"The book of life, or Lamb's book of Life, is the record kept in heaven which contains the names of the faithful and an account of their righteous covenants and deeds. The book of life is the book containing the names of those who shall inherit eternal life; it is the book of*

---

[279] Smith, Joseph Fielding, *Doctrines of Salvation*, 2:21.
[280] 2 Nephi 9:15.
[281] Romans 14:12.

eternal life. It is 'the book of the names of the sanctified, even them of the celestial world.' Names of faithful saints are recorded in the book of life while they are yet in mortality. But those names are blotted out in the event of wickedness." [282]

The Doctrine and Covenants clarifies for us that, in his revelation, John was actually referring to priesthood sealing ordinances:

"Whatsoever you bind on earth shall be bound in heaven, and whatsoever you loose on earth shall be loosed in heaven. Or, in other words, taking a different view of the translation, whatsoever you record on earth shall be recorded in heaven, and whatsoever you do not record on earth shall not be recorded in heaven; for out of the books shall your dead be judged, according to their own works, whether they themselves have attended to the ordinances in their own propria persona, or by the means of their own agents, according to the ordinance which God has prepared for their salvation from before the foundation of the world, according to the records which they have kept concerning their dead." [283]

---

[282] McConkie, Bruce R., *Mormon Doctrine*, p. 97.
[283] D&C 128:8.

The Savior's judgment will be based on our deeds and actions performed in this life. Anyone who has accepted Christ and his gospel, who has been sealed by the power of the priesthood, will receive everlasting life. Anyone who has not accepted him and has not participated in the sealing ordinances will *"remain separately and singly, without exaltation, in their saved condition, to all eternity; and from henceforth are not gods, but are angels of God forever and ever."* [284]

We believe and testify that the Book of Mormon embodies *"the fulness of the gospel of Jesus Christ."* [285] It is a synopsis of Christ's plan of salvation. It is a sacred record of God's dealings with a nation and people who knew and understood what they needed to do to obtain eternal life. If we follow the counsels and teachings outlined in the Book of Mormon, we will become joint-heirs with Christ and inherit the celestial kingdom. This same idea applies to all canon of sacred scripture.

Joseph Smith offered the following significant and reassuring message regarding the final judgment: *"The Great Parent of the universe looks upon the whole*

---

[284] D&C 132:17.
[285] See D&C 20:9.

of the human family with a fatherly care and paternal regard; He views them as His offspring, and without any of those contracted feelings that influence the children of men.... [He] will judge all men, not according to the narrow, contracted notions of men, but, 'according to the deeds done in the body whether they be good or evil,' or whether these deeds were done in England, America, Spain, Turkey, or India. He will judge them, 'not according to what they have not, but according to what they have,' those who have lived without law, will be judged without law, and those who have a law, will be judged by that law.... He will award judgment or mercy to all nations according to their several deserts, their means of obtaining intelligence, the laws by which they are governed, the facilities afforded them of obtaining correct information, and His inscrutable designs in relation to the human family; and when the designs of God shall be made manifest, and the curtain of futurity be withdrawn, we shall all of us eventually have to confess that the Judge of all the earth has done right." [286]

---

[286] Smith, Joseph, *Teachings of the Prophet Joseph Smith*, p. 218.

The book of life is the *"record which is kept in heaven"* [287] containing the names of the righteous. [288] It belongs to the Lamb of God [289] who removes from it the names of sinners [290] but leaves the names of those who overcome the world and are clothed in white raiment.

According to President George Albert Smith: *"If we will serve God, if we will keep his commandments, if we will honor the priesthood that has been conferred upon us, if we will sustain those whom he has called to preside over us, with faith and devotion, when the time shall come for us to go hence we will find our names written in the Lamb's Book of Life, and we will receive at the hands of the Master of heaven and earth that glorious welcome home: 'Well done, thou good and faithful servant: thou hast been faithful over a few things, I will make thee ruler over many things: enter thou into the joy of thy lord.'"* [291] [292]

---

[287] D&C 128:7.

[288] Alma 5:58.

[289] Alma 21:27.

[290] Exodus 32:32, 33.

[291] Matthew 25:21.

[292] Smith, George Albert, *Conference Report*, Oct. 1928, pp. 94, 95.

178

Promise 18

Bless You and Prosper You

"And behold, all that he requires of you is to keep his commandments; and he has promised you that if ye would keep his commandments ye should prosper in the land; and he never doth vary from that which he hath said; therefore, if ye do keep his commandments he doth bless you and prosper you." [293]

I used to ask my seminary students to complete this sentence:

"_____ is the root of all evil."

---

[293] Mosiah 2:22.

Many of them would yell out, "Money. Money is the root of all evil." I would then have them open their scriptures and read: *"For the love of money is the root of all evil: which while some coveted after, they have erred from the faith, and pierced themselves through with many sorrows."* [294] Money itself is not inherently evil, but a love of money can lead to evil purposes.

Contrary to a prevalent and common viewpoint of many members of the Church, wealth and prosperity do not inevitably create a spiritual decline. A predominant and recurring theme throughout the Book of Mormon originates with a statement conveyed by Lehi after arriving to the promised land:

"I have obtained a promise, that inasmuch as those whom the Lord God shall bring out of the land of Jerusalem shall keep his commandments, they shall prosper upon the face of this land; and they shall be kept from all other nations, that they may possess this land unto themselves. And if it so be that they shall keep his commandments they shall be blessed upon the face of this land, and there shall be none to molest them, nor to take away the land of their inheritance; and they shall dwell safely forever." [295]

---

[294] 1 Timothy 6:10.
[295] 2 Nephi 1:9.

The prophets of the Book of Mormon understood that a nation's, as well as an individual's, economy, wealth and prosperity are inevitably connected to the spiritual plane of its people. Nations prosper when spiritual levels rise and deteriorate when the laws of God are persistently disregarded.

The Book of Mormon chronicles the repeated prosperous ascents and subsequent disastrous declines of the great Nephite nation over nine hundred and fifty years. The historical assessment is recorded specifically for our day by Mormon and Moroni who not only watched first-hand the thorough destruction of the Nephite nation, but who also witnessed, through historic records and sacred writings, the complete drawn-out and decisive drama of the prosperity cycle.

Included in those sacred writings is the history of another civilization, the Jaredite nation, which existed for almost two thousand years. The Jaredite record contains accounts of two of the longest periods of peace and prosperity ever recorded in human history. Under the righteous reign of King Emer, the Jaredite nation judiciously observed and obeyed the laws of God, and *"they became exceedingly rich."* [296] Generations later they abandoned their peace and

---

[296] Ether 9:16-23.

their prosperity when *"an exceeding great wickedness spread over the face of the land."* [297]

Peace was eventually restored, and prosperity reclaimed under King Levi. These prosperous and peaceful times continued uninterrupted for five generations. Moroni revealed to us the secret of their wealth and prosperity when he declared that they *"did that which was right in the sight of the Lord."* [298]

"And never could be a people more blessed than were they, and more prospered by the hand of the Lord. And they were in a land that was choice above all lands, for the Lord had spoken it." [299]

Throughout the Book of Mormon, prophets who knew of the promise of prosperity given to Lehi often reminded their people of the conditions required and the blessings offered to those living in a land of promise. *"And this was their faith, that by so doing God would prosper them in the land, or in other words, if they were faithful in keeping the commandments of God that he would prosper them in the land; yea, warn*

---

[297] Ether 2:26.

[298] Ether 10:19.

[299] Ether 10:28.

them to flee, or to prepare for war, according to their danger." [300]

King Benjamin affirmed to his people that all that God *"requires of you is to keep his commandments; and he has promised you that if ye would keep his commandments ye should prosper in the land; and he never doth vary from that which he hath said; therefore, if ye do keep his commandments he doth bless you and prosper you."* [301]

Jarom attributed his success in battle to this same promise: *"And thus being prepared to meet the Lamanites, they did not prosper against us. But the word of the Lord was verified, which he spake unto our fathers, saying that: Inasmuch as ye will keep my commandments ye shall prosper in the land."* [302]

Alma pled with his son: *"O remember, remember, my son Helaman, how strict are the commandments of God. And he said: If ye will keep my commandments ye shall prosper in the land—but if ye*

---

[300] Alma 48:15.

[301] Mosiah 2:22.

[302] Jarom 1:9.

keep not his commandments ye shall be cut off from his presence." [303]

The ancient prophets of the promised land considered wealth a direct blessing made possible through obedience to God's law. Prosperity was not seen as a curse but a benediction. Wealth, in the hands of an obedient people, provided greater opportunities for spiritual expression and development. This is the philosophy conveyed in the Book of Jacob:

"Think of your brethren like unto yourselves, and be familiar with all and free with your substance, that they may be rich like unto you.

"But before ye seek for riches, seek ye for the kingdom of God.

"And after ye have obtained a hope in Christ ye shall obtain riches, if ye seek them; and ye will seek them for the intent to do good—to clothe the naked, and to feed the hungry, and to liberate the captive, and administer relief to the sick and the afflicted." [304]

Mormon observed a particular behavior among the prosperous Nephites during the time of Alma:

---

[303] Alma 37:3.
[304] Jacob 2:17-19.

"And thus, in their prosperous circumstances, they did not send away any who were naked, or that were hungry, or that were athirst, or that were sick, or that had not been nourished; and they did not set their hearts upon riches; therefore they were liberal to all, both old and young, both bond and free, both male and female, whether out of the church or in the church, having no respect to persons as to those who stood in need.

"And thus they did prosper and become far more wealthy than those who did not belong to their church." [305]

The Book of Mormon also tells us of Nephites who "Notwithstanding their riches, or their strength, or their prosperity, they were not lifted up in the pride of their eyes; neither were they slow to remember the Lord their God; but they did humble themselves exceedingly before him." [306]

The problem with prosperity arises when we forget Jacob's counsel and take for granted the blessings of abundance earned through obedience. We easily fall victim to the prosperity cycle when pride leads us to rebellion, rebellion to suffering, and

---

[305] Alma 1:30, 31.
[306] Alma 62:49.

suffering to repentance. In turn, repentance returns us to obedience and obedience to prosperity. This cycle can become a repetitive pattern if we are not grounded in the gospel. The Book of Helaman warns us against unsteadiness and hardening our hearts:

"And thus we can behold how false, and also the unsteadiness of the hearts of the children of men; yea, we can see that the Lord in his great infinite goodness doth bless and prosper those who put their trust in him.

"Yea, and we may see at the very time when he doth prosper his people, yea, in the increase of their fields, their flocks and their herds, and in gold, and in silver, and in all manner of precious things of every kind and art; sparing their lives, and delivering them out of the hands of their enemies; softening the hearts of their enemies that they should not declare wars against them; yea, and in fine, doing all things for the welfare and happiness of his people; yea, then is the time that they do harden their hearts, and do forget the Lord their God, and do trample under their feet the Holy One—yea, and this because of their ease, and their exceedingly great prosperity." [307]

---

[307] Helaman 12:1, 2.

The nations established in the promised land have been blessed with a surplus of resources. This is an abundantly rich land. To enjoy a truly prosperous lifestyle, those who live here must possess a great love of God and fellow men or the prosperity cycle will renew its downward spiral. Roger W. Babson, author of *"Fundamentals of Prosperity"* made the following incisive remark:

"What causes these fluctuations in business and prices? Statistics show that crises are caused by spiritual causes, rather than financial, and prosperity is the result of righteousness rather than of material things. These spiritual forces are the true fundamentals of prosperity." [308]

The Book of Mormon, a poignant record portraying the moral decline and eventual complete destruction of a civilization, speaks to us as a constant warning:

"They were once a delightsome people, and they had Christ for their shepherd; yea, they were led even by God the Father.

"But now, behold, they are led about by Satan, even as chaff is driven before the wind, or as a vessel

---

[308] Babson, Roger W., *Fundamentals of Prosperity*, p. 73.

is tossed about upon the waves, without sail or anchor, or without anything wherewith to steer her; and even as she is, so are they." [309]

The promise of prosperity mentioned in the Book of Mormon has never been repealed or withdrawn. In plain and simple language, it declares: *"Inasmuch as ye shall keep the commandments of God ye shall prosper in the land."* [310] This promise is applicable to individuals as well as to families as well as to entire nations. The blessing is promised to the obedient. The loss of blessing falls to those who disregard the laws of God. [311]

The pattern of prosperity and poverty is repeated throughout the pages of the Book of Mormon like a recurring melody. The promise of prosperity will emerge as we begin to *"liken all scriptures unto us, that it might be for our profit and learning."* [312] As we interweave ourselves into the lessons and stories in this sacred book and accept that God is speaking directly to us, we can then feel and understand his promise to us:

---

[309] Mormon 5:17, 18.

[310] Alma 36:30.

[311] See Deuteronomy 11:26-28.

[312] 1 Nephi 19:23.

"But behold, my son, this is not all; for ye ought to know as I do know, that inasmuch as ye shall keep the commandments of God ye shall prosper in the land; and ye ought to know also, that inasmuch as ye will not keep the commandments of God ye shall be cut off from his presence. Now this is according to his word." [313]

Heber C. Kimball has added this counsel to us: "Brethren and sisters, remember all your duties and perform them, and the Lord Almighty will bless you and prosper you in all things which you set your hands to do." [314]

---

[313] Alma 36:30.

[314] Kimball, Heber C., *Journal of Discourses*, vol. 9.

Promise 19

Dwell Safely

"But, behold, all nations, kindreds, tongues, and people shall dwell safely in the Holy One of Israel if it so be that they will repent." [315]

After Nephi had read certain passages from the brass plates of Laban, his brothers asked him, *"What meaneth these things which ye have read?"* [316] As Nephi attempts to enlighten his brothers on both the temporal and spiritual interpretation of the scriptures, he tells them that *"the time soon cometh that the*

---

[315] 1 Nephi 22:28.
[316] 1 Nephi 22:1.

fulness of the wrath of God shall be poured out upon all the children of men." [317]

Nephi then warns his brothers that *"these things must shortly come; yea, even blood, and fire, and vapor of smoke must come; and it must needs be on the face of this earth."* [318]

Nephi also tells his brothers that *"all these things must come according to the flesh"* but that *"all nations, kindreds, tongues, and people may dwell safely in the Holy One of Israel if they will repent."* [319] Nephi hesitates at this point to speak any more *"concerning these things"* but he encourages his brothers to *"consider that the things which have been written upon the plates of brass are true."* [320]

It would certainly seem that the key to the promise to *"dwell safely in the Holy One of Israel"* is contingent on our willingness to repent. Jacob, a brother of Nephi, taught that *"the days of the children of men were prolonged, according to the will of God, that they might repent while in the flesh; wherefore,*

---

[317] 1 Nephi 22:16.
[318] 1 Nephi 22:18.
[319] 1 Nephi 22:27, 28.
[320] 1 Nephi 22:29, 30.

their state became a state of probation, and their time was lengthened, according to the commandments which the Lord God gave unto the children of men." [321] The explicit intent of this probationary period was to give everyone the maximum possibility to repent. *"For he gave commandment that all men must repent; for he showed unto all men that they were lost."* [322]

Most everyone who has reached the age of accountability knows right from wrong and there is plenty of scripture, counsel and instruction to provide us with a working knowledge of righteousness and wickedness. King Benjamin conveyed to the people of his time that he could not tell them *"all the things whereby ye may commit sin, for there are diverse ways and means, even so many that I cannot number them."* [323]

The standard of righteousness is repentance. The criterion of righteousness, (as well as of wickedness, for that matter) is not one of position, but one of direction. No one other than the Savior is exempt from the need to repent. The resurrected Christ personally declared to the Nephite nation: *"Wo unto the*

---

[321] 2 Nephi 2:21.

[322] Ibid.

[323] Mosiah 4:29.

inhabitants of the whole earth, except they shall repent." [324]

We cannot argue that others need repentance more than we do. Hugh Nibley wrote that *"until we have reached the shore, no one is home safe; a swimmer can drown fifty feet from the shore as easily as a mile from it; and in this life, none have reached the shore, for it is a probation right up until the last."* [325] Christ bore record to the Nephites that *"the Father commandeth all men, everywhere, to repent and believe in me."* [326]

We cannot argue that our sin is better than someone else's sin. It is not a question of degree. A small sin will keep a person out of heaven as effectively as a great one. Which would you believe is more inexcusable, the sins of a righteous person who has fallen, or the sins of a wicked person who has repented? Helaman teaches us that *"blessed are they who will repent... for these are they that shall be saved."* [327] The Book of Ether, on the other hand,

---

[324] 3 Nephi 9:2.
[325] Nibley, Hugh, *Prophetic Book of Mormon*, Deseret Book Company, 1989.
[326] 3 Nephi 11:32.
[327] Helaman 12:23.

explains that *"we are unworthy before [God]; because of the fall our natures have become evil continually."* [328]

Ezekiel, the Old Testament prophet, conveys the message that our righteous state or our wicked state is not determined so much by whose side we have professed to be on but rather, by which direction we are moving. Ezekiel explains to us that: *"If the wicked will turn from all his sins that he hath committed, and keep all my statutes, and do that which is lawful and right, he shall surely live, he shall not die. All his transgressions that he hath committed, they shall not be mentioned unto him.... But when the righteous turneth away from his righteousness, and committeth iniquity, and doeth according to all the abominations that the wicked man doeth, shall he live? All his righteousness that he hath done shall not be mentioned."* [329]

In other words, when a person who has lived an unrighteous life repents and turns toward the Lord, that person is considered righteous, and when a righteous person with a long list of moral and honorable accomplishments turns wicked, that person will be

---

[328] Ether 3:2.
[329] See Ezekiel 18:21-26.

considered unrighteous. As Hugh Nibley explains: *"The person on the top step facing down is in worse condition than one on a bottom step facing up."* [330]

In the October 2017 General Conference, Jeffery R. Holland [331] related a comment made by Leo Tolstoy. In response to criticism he was given for not living as unwaveringly as some thought he should, Tolstoy wrote: *"I am trying to live out the truth I proclaim.... If I know the way home [but] am walking along it drunkenly, is it any less the right way because I am staggering from side to side?"* [332]

The purpose of the Book of Mormon is to convince us that Jesus is the Christ. Our hope for eternal life hinges on that proposition. The message of the Book of Mormon is the message of the gospel, a message of repentance and forgiveness and dwelling safely in the Holy One of Israel.

---

[330] Nibley, Hugh, *Prophetic Book of Mormon*, Deseret Book Company, 1989.
[331] See Holland, Jeffery R., *Be Ye Therefore Perfect—Eventually.* Conference Report, 2017.
[332] Tolstoy, Leo, *The New Way,* Spiritual Writing, Charles E. Moore, 2006, pp. 81, 82.

Promise 20

Free from Captivity

"Behold, this is a choice land, and whatsoever nation shall possess it shall be free from bondage, and from captivity, and from all other nations under heaven, if they will but serve the God of the land, who is Jesus Christ, who hath been manifested by the things which we have written." [333]

The land we live in, the land of the restored gospel of Jesus Christ, exists for one specific purpose. It is a unique function of the United States of America. According to Mark E. Petersen: *"There is a United States only because God planned to restore the gospel in the last days and he had to have a free country in*

---

[333] Ether 2:12.

which to do it, with freedom of worship, freedom of the press, freedom of speech, and freedom of assembly." [334]

The Book of Mormon affirms that this land is choice above all other lands. What makes this country a choice land is its purpose and destiny. No other nation on earth has such an important purpose in the eternal plan than ours.

Joseph F. Smith has acknowledged that: *"This great American nation the Almighty raised up by the power of his omnipotent hand, that it might be possible in the latter days for the kingdom of God to be established in the earth.... His hand has been over this nation, and it is his purpose and design to enlarge it—make it glorious above all others, and to give it dominion, and power over the earth, to the end that those who are kept in bondage and serfdom may be brought to the enjoyment of the fullest freedom and liberty of conscience possible for intelligent men to exercise in the earth."* [335]

---

[334] Petersen, Mark E., *America—World Leader*, BYU Speeches, July 4, 1976.

[335] Smith, Joseph F., *Gospel Doctrine*, Deseret Book, p. 409.

The powerful role that this country is destined to play is to help the world prepare for the second coming of Christ. That is the specific purpose for which this nation was set up. This country was established, under the hand of God, as a land of freedom, where he could restore his gospel in preparation for the second coming of the Lord Jesus Christ.

The First Presidency, in 1973, urged *"members of the Church and all Americans to begin now to reflect more intently on the meaning and importance of the Constitution, and of adherence to its principles.... In these challenging days, when there are so many influences which would divert us, there is a need to rededicate ourselves to the lofty principles and practices of our Founding Fathers."* [336]

Maintaining this country's freedom is an ongoing responsibility. Liberty and democracy are worthy of our continued and constant support. Freedom has always been part of the American dream and freedom has been promised on the condition that the people in this land serve the God of this land. The Book of Mormon reminds us that *"this land is consecrated unto him whom he shall bring. And if it so*

---

[336] Message of the First Presidency, *Church News*, September 22, 1973, p. 3.

be that they shall serve him according to the commandments which he hath given, it shall be a land of liberty unto them; wherefore, they shall never be brought down into captivity; if so, it shall be because of iniquity; for if iniquity shall abound, cursed shall be the land for their sakes, but unto the righteous it shall be blessed forever." [337]

The message of the restored gospel that we bear is to be conveyed to the world from this nation. The gospel will flourish only in an atmosphere of freedom. As citizens of this purposeful and predestined land, it is our responsibility to maintain and strengthen our sacred freedoms.

President J. Reuben Clark has stated: *"The Constitution of the United States is a great and treasured part of my religion.... The overturning, or the material changing, or the distortion of any fundamental principle of our constitutional government would thus do violence to my religion.... My faith teaches me that the Constitution is an inspired document drawn by the hands of men whom God raised up for that very purpose; that God has given His approval of the Government set up under the Constitution 'for the rights and protection of all flesh, according to just and*

---

[337] 2 Nephi 1:7.

holy principles': that the constitutional 'principle of freedom in maintaining rights and privileges, belongs to all mankind, and is justifiable before' the Lord. [338].... So far as my knowledge goes, this is the only government now on the earth to which God has given such an approval. It is His plan for the government of free men." [339]

To maintain the liberties we cherish in the Church and kingdom of God established in this land, we should commit to serve the God of this land and to live according to the truths that he has revealed. President John Taylor said: "It has been asked whether this kingdom will fail. I tell you in the name of Israel's God it will not fail. I tell you in the name of Israel's God it will roll forth and that the things spoken of by the holy prophets in relation to it will receive their fulfillment." [340]

Our nation has a prophetic history established on a spiritual foundation. It is the Lord's center of operations in the last days. It is our responsibility to strengthen and safeguard the freedoms that will allow the gospel to move forward toward its ordained purpose.

---

[338] See D&C 101:77, 98:5.

[339] Clark, J. Reuben, *Stand Fast by Our Constitution*, pp. 7, 172.

[340] Taylor, John, *Gospel Kingdom*, p. 137.

President Harold B. Lee has proclaimed: *"The Constitution will stand even if it must be saved by the elders of this Church. This nation, founded on the principles laid down by men whom God raised up, will never fail. I have faith in America, and you and I must have faith in America if we understand the teachings of the gospel of the Lord Jesus Christ."* [341]

The Constitution of the United States of America is ordained of God and was brought about through men whom God raised up for that purpose. We should re-dedicate ourselves to the principles and practices that will safeguard our priceless freedom. Our liberties as a church and nation are dependent on us being obedient to the God of this land.

Brigham Young said: *"When the day comes in which the Kingdom of God will bear rule, the flag of the United States will proudly flutter unsullied on the flag staff of liberty and equal rights, without a spot to sully its fair surface; the glorious flag our fathers have bequeathed to us will then be unfurled to the breeze by those who have power to hoist it aloft and defend its sanctity."* [342]

---

[341] Lee, Harold B., Deseret News, October 27, 1973.

[342] Young, Brigham, *Discourses of Brigham Young*, Deseret Book, p. 360.

Promise 21

Raised unto Life Eternal

"And what is it that ye shall hope for? Behold I say unto you that ye shall have hope through the atonement of Christ and the power of his resurrection, to be raised unto life eternal, and this because of your faith in him according to the promise." [343]

All of us are spirit children of Heavenly Father, beginning with Christ who was our Father's first begotten son in the spirit. In our pre-mortal world, Jesus was appointed to be the Son of God in the flesh and live a life free of sin. His purpose and mission on this earth was to satisfy the demands of justice for the sins of all

---

[343] Moroni 7:41.

of God's children. Lehi proclaimed that mission and purpose nearly six centuries before Christ would come, saying that Jesus would offer *"himself a sacrifice for sin, to answer the ends of the law, unto all those who have a broken heart and a contrite spirit; and unto none else can the ends of the law be answered."* [344]

He also declared that *"there is no flesh that can dwell in the presence of God, save it be through the merits, and mercy, and grace of the Holy Messiah."* [345]

All of Father's children can be edified by the Spirit of God, but we are also all tempted by Satan. Through the exercise of our free agency, we actually exclude ourselves from God's presence and cannot be re-admitted unaided or on our own since giving in to temptation renders us unclean. All flesh, being carnal, sensual, and devilish, is driven out from the kingdom of God, because *"no unclean thing can enter into his kingdom."* [346]

To allow us to return to our Father in heaven, an atonement for our sins was provided by the only one who was not banished from our Father's presence and the only one who never yielded to temptation: Jesus

---

[344] 2 Nephi 2:7.
[345] Ibid., 8.
[346] 3 Nephi 27:19.

Christ. Jesus later described the suffering he underwent in these expressive words:

"I, God, have suffered these things for all, that they might not suffer if they would repent;

"But if they would not repent they must suffer even as I;

"Which suffering caused myself, even God, the greatest of all, to tremble because of pain, and to bleed at every pore, and to suffer both body and spirit—and would that I might not drink the bitter cup, and shrink—

"Nevertheless, glory be to the Father, and I partook and finished my preparations unto the children of men." [347]

Jesus paid the price to provide the means for us to find forgiveness, through faith and repentance, and to reap the blessings of eternal life. This is possible only through the incomparable offering of the atonement.

Jacob taught us that Christ *"cometh into the world that he may save all men if they will hearken unto his voice; for behold, he suffereth the pains of all men, yea, the pains of every living creature, both men,*

---

[347] D&C 19:16-19.

women, and children, who belong to the family of Adam." [348]

The physical pain and mental suffering our Savior was required to endure had to be sufficiently strong and intense to compensate for the sins of every single one of God's other children.

John teaches us that *"the hour is coming, in the which all that are in the graves shall hear his voice,*

"And shall come forth; they that have done good, unto the resurrection of life; and they that have done evil, unto the resurrection of damnation." [349]

President Joseph Fielding Smith explained that *"the destiny of man is to pass through three estates. First, he existed as a spirit in the presence of God. Second, by and through the goodness and mercy of the Father, he is privileged to come to earth, here or somewhere else, and pass through mortality partaking of all the vicissitudes of which the mortal life has to offer. The third and final estate is that of the resurrection, the coming forth from the grave after death, the spirit and body being inseparably united.*

---

[348] 2 Nephi 9:21.
[349] John 5:28, 29.

This is immortality. This gift will be given to every mortal creature whether he be good or bad, whether or not he seeks it." [350]

The apostle Paul succinctly and accurately described immortality when he stated: *"As in Adam all die, even so in Christ shall all be made alive."* [351] Having faith in Christ is not a requirement for receiving the gift of resurrection.

Joseph Fielding Smith differentiates immortality from eternal life in these words: *"The distinction between eternal life, as received by the faithful, and immortality, obtained by both the faithful and unfaithful, is shown in the words of the Lord to Moses: 'And behold, this is my work and my glory—to bring to pass the immortality and eternal life of man.' The conjunction clearly separates the two thoughts. It explains that the Lord is giving to the vast majority of men, those who will not be obedient, the blessing of immortality; and to those who will serve him, the blessing of eternal life."* [352]

---

[350] Smith, Joseph Fielding, *The Progress of Man,* Genealogical Society of Utah, 1936, p. 507.

[351] 1 Corinthians 15:22.

[352] Smith, Joseph Fielding, *The Way to Perfection*, Genealogical Society of Utah, 1935, p. 329.

Death is but another phase of our immortal lives. We are living a portion of a life that reaches into eternity after our spirit leaves its physical body. Eternal progress suggests that we should be trying to live with the resolves and purposes we want to carry with us into eternity. This is the purpose of the Church—that with the aid and guidance of the gospel of Jesus Christ, we can practice immortality today and begin to live lives worthy of eternity.

Moroni teaches us through the words of his prayer that God *"hast prepared a house for man, yea, even among the mansions of thy Father, in which man might have a more excellent hope; wherefore man must hope, or he cannot receive an inheritance in the place which thou hast prepared."* [353] Jacob noted that: *"We search the prophets, and we have many revelations and the spirit of prophecy; and having all these witnesses we obtain a hope, and our faith becometh unshaken."* [354]

Mormon, writing on faith, hope, and charity, puts both immortality and eternal life in clear perspective: *"What is it that ye shall hope for? Behold I*

---

[353] Ether 12:32.
[354] Jacob 4:6.

say unto you that ye shall have hope through the atonement of Christ and the power of his resurrection, to be raised unto life eternal." [355]

Eternal life is the greatest gift of God. It comprises the fullness of God's kingdom and will allow us to dwell with the Father and the Son. We become joint-heirs with Christ in receiving the fullness of the Father's kingdom. [356]

If we meet the criteria for receiving this characteristic of Christ's atonement, we are born again. We are forgiven of our sins and become a new creature in Christ, taking on his divine nature. As such we obtain peace of conscience and are filled with joy; [357] and have *"no more disposition to do evil, but to do good continually."* [358] These results can be immediate.

In the Book of Mormon, Amulek encourages us to *"come forth and bring fruit unto repentance.... for behold now is the time and the day of your salvation; and therefore, if ye will repent and harden not your*

---

[355] Moroni 7:41.

[356] See Romans 8:14-17.

[357] See Mosiah 4:3.

[358] Mosiah 5:2.

hearts, immediately shall the great plan of redemption be brought about unto you." [359]

Joseph Smith wrote of life's eternal value and significance, stating: *"But if this life is all, then why this constant toiling, why this continual warfare, and why this unceasing trouble? But this life is not all; the voice of reason, the language of inspiration, and the Spirit of the living God, our Creator, teaches us, as we hold the record of truth in our hands, that this is not the case, that this is not so; for, the heavens declare the glory of a God, and the firmament showeth His handiwork; and a moment's reflection is sufficient to teach every man of common intelligence, that all these are not the mere productions of chance, nor could they be supported by any power less than an Almighty hand."* [360]

Faith in an eternal existence creates unimaginable opportunities. Obert C. Tanner suggests that we can live today, not just in how we speak, but in genuinely being sincere with others. We can live today not with just outwardly spoken prayers, but by our secret inner prayers that no one hears. We can live today not just by controlling our outward impulses, but by living a life where lust cannot exist. We can live today

---

[359] Alma 34: 30, 31.

[360] Smith, Joseph, *Teachings of the Prophet Joseph Smith,* Deseret News Press, 1938, p. 56.

not just by keeping our word, but by being completely trustworthy. We can live today not just by serving others through our labor and means, but by deeply loving those we serve. We can live today not just with an outward compliance to gospel practices, but with an inward desire to repent and walk humbly before God. [361]

The touchstone for living an eternal life is distinctly noted in the following scripture: *"We know that we have passed from death unto life, because we love the brethren. He that loveth not his brother abideth in death."* [362]

Christian author George A. Gordon put the matter of immortality and eternal life in the hands of God. He wrote:

"For myself, I ground all hope in God. Whether, therefore, we wake, or sleep, we are the Lord's. He gave us being, and if it shall so please him he will continue us in being the endless partakers of his life and joy. As old Marcus Aurelius said, 'It is good to die if there is a God, and sad to live if there is not.' The whole

---

[361] See Tanner, Obert C., *Christ's Ideals for Living*, Deseret Book, 1955.
[362] 1 John 3:14.

question rests with our maker, who is our Heavenly Father and whose character has been expressed with sovereign beauty and power by the Lord Jesus Christ." 363

A verse from First Corinthians suggests that we can beautify our inner lives and make them worthy of heaven:

"And as we have borne the image of the earthly, we shall also bear the image of the heavenly." 364

363 Gordon, George A., *"All Hope Rests in God," Treasury of the Christian Faith,* Association Press, N.Y., 1949, p. 425.
364 1 Corinthians 15:49.

Promise 22

Consolation in Affliction

"But behold, I, Jacob, would speak unto you that are pure in heart. Look unto God with firmness of mind, and pray unto him with exceeding faith, and he will console you in your afflictions, and he will plead your cause, and send down justice upon those who seek your destruction." [365]

The Savior of all humanity uttered a tender and heart-rending supplication in a revelation given through the prophet Joseph Smith in 1831: *"Listen to him who is the advocate with the Father, who is pleading your*

---

[365] Jacob 3:1.

cause before him—saying: Father, behold the sufferings and death of him who did no sin, in whom thou wast well pleased; behold the blood of thy Son which was shed, the blood of him whom thou gavest that thyself might be glorified; wherefore, Father, spare these my brethren that believe on my name, that they may come unto me and have everlasting life." [366]

The Book of Mormon, an additional witness of Jesus Christ, invites us to experience the mercy and love that our Redeemer imparts to everyone who will accept him as their Savior. The invitation that Alma made known to the people of his time is still open to all of us today. *"Behold, he sendeth an invitation unto all men, for the arms of mercy are extended towards them, and he saith: Repent, and I will receive you. Yea, he saith: Come unto me and ye shall partake of the fruit of the tree of life; yea, ye shall eat and drink of the bread and the waters of life freely."* [367]

Certainly, afflictions and hardships fall like torrential rains in the lives of every mortal travelling the terrestrial road toward eternity. The occasional sunshine that breaks through the tempest, offering us

---

[366] D&C 45:3-5.
[367] Alma 5:33, 34.

respite from our worries and unrest, is a blessing offered from beyond this world.

Jesus extends his own personal directive to us:

"Come unto me, all ye that labour and are heavy laden, and I will give you rest.

"Take my yoke upon you, and learn of me; for I am meek and lowly in heart: and ye shall find rest unto your souls.

"For my yoke is easy, and my burden is light." 368

As children of God, we are entitled to the Spirit of God. The gift of the Holy Ghost is bestowed on all those who unite themselves with the kingdom of God. The Holy Ghost is not only a revelator, a sanctifier, and a sealer. He is also a comforter and we are entitled to the comfort and consolation offered through the word of God.

As the Nephites gathered for their final battles, Mormon laments the loss of the fair sons and

---

368 Matthew 11:28-30.

daughters of Nephi, reminding them (and us) that Jesus *"stood with open arms to receive you!"* [369]

Mormon's son, Moroni, finishing the account of the Jaredite civilization, urges us *"to seek this Jesus of whom the prophets and apostles have written."* [370]

There is consolation in Jesus Christ. He is more powerful than the evils of this world. He is stronger than Satan whose determination is to spiritually destroy our souls. Through Christ we can not only cope with the harsh conditions of life; we can survive and thrive successfully and with power.

The Book of Mormon encourages us to *"Remember that it is upon the rock of our Redeemer, who is Christ, the Son of God, that you must build your foundation; that when the devil shall send forth his mighty winds, yea, his shafts in the whirlwind, yea, when all his hail and his mighty storm shall beat upon you, it shall have no power over you to drag you down to the gulf of misery and endless wo, because of the rock upon which ye are built."* [371]

---

[369] Mormon 6:17.

[370] Ether 12:41.

[371] Helaman 5:12.

The power of Christ's atonement is sufficient to overcome the evil and injustices of this world. The Book of Mormon demonstrates how we may obtain that power for our trying circumstances and situations. The Book of Mormon is replete with illustrations and standards that can convey the consolation of Christ into our hearts.

Joseph Smith taught us that *"without the idea of the existence of the attribute of justice in the Deity, men could not have confidence sufficient to place themselves under his guidance and direction. For they would be filled with fear and doubt lest the Judge of all the earth would not do right... It is through the exercise of this attribute that the faithful in Christ Jesus are delivered out of the hands of those who seek their destruction: for if God were not to come out in swift judgment against the workers of iniquity and the powers of darkness, his saints could not be saved; for it is by judgment that the Lord delivers his saints out of the hands of all their enemies, and those who reject the gospel of our Lord Jesus Christ."* [372]

It may be difficult at times to identify with such a great promise. As followers of Jesus Christ we should embrace the concept that the Lord knows our hearts

---

[372] Smith, Joseph, *Lectures on Faith*, 4:13, 14.

and will plead our specific and personal cause and contention and will deliver justice to those who seek to harm us.

Bruce R. McConkie has written: *"Because the Holy Spirit speaks peace to the hearts of weary and disconsolate mortals, he is called the Comforter. He brings peace and solace, love and quiet enjoyment, the joy of redemption and the hope of eternal life."* [373]

Christ suffered for all, but he particularly pleads the plight of the righteous who repent and follow his teachings. [374] The intercession of the Son of God is offered to those who have a broken heart and a contrite spirit—to those who have become the children of Christ. [375]

The ancient prophet Abinadi declared: *"Whosoever has heard the words of the prophets, yea, all the holy prophets who have prophesied concerning the coming of the Lord—I say unto you, that all those who have hearkened unto their words, and believed that the Lord would redeem his people, and have looked forward to that day for a remission of their sins,*

---

[373] McConkie, Bruce R., *A New Witness*. Deseret Book. P. 268.
[374] See 2 Nephi 9:21; Alma 11:40; D&C 18:11-12; 19:16-17; 38:4.
[375] See 2 Nephi 2:6, 7.

I say unto you, that these are his seed, or they are the heirs of the kingdom of God.

"For these are they whose sins he has borne, these are they for whom he has died, to redeem them from their transgressions." [376]

Clearly, there is sin in this world. The Book of Mormon teaches of the chains of hell and the captivity of the devil. It also teaches that there is power to overcome sin in the atonement of Jesus Christ.

As Moroni watched the destruction of the Nephite civilization, he wrote these words to *"all the ends of the earth—*

"Come unto Christ, and be perfected in him, and deny yourselves of all ungodliness; and if ye shall deny yourselves of all ungodliness, and love God with all your might, mind and strength, then is his grace sufficient for you." [377]

---

[376] Mosiah 15:11, 12.
[377] Moroni 10:24, 32.

Promise 23

Miracles, Signs and Wonders

"And now, O all ye that have imagined up unto yourselves a god who can do no miracles, I would ask of you, have all these things passed, of which I have spoken? Has the end come yet? Behold I say unto you, Nay; and God has not ceased to be a God of miracles." [378]

Miracles have always existed among people with faith.

"For I am God, and mine arm is not shortened; and I will show miracles, signs, and wonders, unto all those who believe on my name.

---

[378] Mormon 9:15.

"And whoso shall ask it in my name in faith, they shall cast out devils; they shall heal the sick; they shall cause the blind to receive their sight, and the deaf to hear, and the dumb to speak, and the lame to walk." [379]

Miracles are performed through faith and righteousness. [380] Miracles are not manifest without a solid foundation of faithfulness. [381] Miracles are the effects and consequence of faith and obedience. Manifestations are characteristic of Paul's teachings: *"And God hath set some in the church, first apostles, secondarily prophets, thirdly teachers, after that miracles, then gifts of healings, helps, governments, diversities of tongues."* [382]

Miracles accompany and testify of the Lord's divine work. They are signs which follow true believers. [383] The miracles Jesus performed during his mortal ministry are evidence of his divine calling. [384]

---

[379] D&C 35:8, 9.

[380] See 2 Nephi 26:13; Mosiah 8:18.

[381] See Ether 12:15, 16, 18.

[382] 1 Corinthians 12:28.

[383] See Mormon 9:20-25; Mark 16:14-20.

[384] See Helaman 16:4; 4 Nephi 31; John 3:2.

Jesus' ministry was characterized by many signs, wonders, and miracles. Following Christ's crucifixion, the apostles demonstrated the divine nature of their callings through miracles which exceeded the common characteristics of mortal beings. The Book of Mormon reveals: *"There was not any man who could do a miracle in the name of Jesus, save he were cleansed every whit from his iniquity."* [385]

Gifts of the Spirit have been a fundamental part of the church of Jesus Christ from its foundation. The Book of Mormon affirms that miracles will continue to exist in the church so long as God's children continue to believe in them. *"For it is by faith that miracles are wrought; and it is by faith that angels appear and minister unto men; wherefore if these things have ceased, wo be unto the children of men, for it is because of unbelief, and all is vain."* [386]

Miracles will, however, cease when wickedness prevails among a people. [387] The Book of Mormon was reserved for *"a day when it shall be said that miracles are done away."* [388] Miracles did end as apostasy in Christ's church advanced. The core root of this

---

[385] 3 Nephi 8:1.

[386] Moroni 7:37.

[387] Mormon 1:13.

[388] Mormon 8:26.

interruption of signs and wonders was the transgression of God's laws.

The denial of miracles is a powerful indicator of apostasy. The Book of Mormon teaches that churches will be built up that *"deny the power of God, the Holy One of Israel; and they say unto the people: Hearken unto us, and hear ye our precept; for behold there is no God today, for the Lord and the Redeemer hath done his work, and he hath given his power unto men;*

"Behold, hearken ye unto my precept; if they shall say there is a miracle wrought by the hand of the Lord, believe it not; for this day he is not a God of miracles; he hath done his work." [389]

This belief is contrary to the commandment and promise that the Savior gave to his apostles after his resurrection. Mark tells us that Christ commanded them to go *"into all the world, and preach the gospel to every creature.*

"He that believeth and is baptized shall be saved; but he that believeth not shall be damned.

---

[389] 2 Nephi 28:5, 6.

"And these signs shall follow them that believe; In my name shall they cast out devils; they shall speak with new tongues;

"They shall take up serpents; and if they drink any deadly thing, it shall not hurt them; they shall lay hands on the sick, and they shall recover." [390]

Miracles are promised to those who believe and obey. To the world, they may seem to be merely odd and unusual phenomena; to the faithful, they are manifestations of the power and purposes of God. Moroni boldly promises to *"show unto you a God of miracles, even the God of Abraham, and the God of Isaac, and the God of Jacob; and it is that same God who created the heavens and the earth, and all things that in them are."* [391]

Moroni declared that those *"who deny the revelations of God, and say that they are done away, that there are no revelations, nor prophecies, nor gifts, nor healing, nor speaking with tongues, and the interpretation of tongues...*

---

[390] Mark 16:15-18.
[391] Mormon 9:11.

"He that denieth these things, knoweth not the gospel of Christ; yea, he has not read the scriptures; if so, he does not understand them.

"For do we not read that God is the same yesterday, today, and for ever; and in him there is no variableness neither shadow of changing?

"And now, if ye have imagined up unto yourselves a god who doth vary, and in him there is shadow of changing, then have ye imagined up unto yourselves a god who is not a God of miracles." [392]

Miracles should not, however, be considered as reliable evidence or unfailing proof of divine power. The Lord revealed the following warning through the prophet Joseph Smith:

"Wherefore, beware lest ye are deceived; and that ye may not be deceived, seek ye earnestly the best gifts, always remembering for what they are given.

"For verily I say unto you, they are given for the benefit of those who love me and keep all my commandments, and him that seeketh so to do, that all may be benefited that seeketh or that asketh of me,

---

[392] Moroni 9:7-10.

that asketh and not for a sign that he may consume it upon his lusts." [393]

Evil powers also work wonders for the purpose of deception. Miracles by themselves, without additional evidence, do not constitute a conclusive confirmation of divine power. Egypt's magicians imitated, in some degree, the powerful miracles of Moses. False, counterfeit miracles can be performed through evil designs. [394]

John the Revelator warned of evil powers misleading the honest in heart through apparent supernatural feats. He witnessed *"the spirits of devils working miracles."* [395] The Savior warns his followers against spiritual fraud and deception: *"There shall arise false Christs, and false prophets, and shall shew great signs and wonders; insomuch that, if it were possible, they shall deceive the very elect."* [396]

Miracles that are a manifestation of the Holy Spirit are always performed in the name of Jesus Christ

---

[393] D&C 46:8, 9.

[394] See Revelation 13:13, 14; 16:14; 19:20.

[395] Ibid.

[396] Matthew 24:24.

and they are performed for the purpose of fostering faith and furthering God's work and glory.

Promise 24

Alive in Christ

"For behold that all little children are alive in Christ, and also all they that are without the law. For the power of redemption cometh on all them that have no law; wherefore, he that is not condemned, or he that is under no condemnation, cannot repent; and unto such baptism availeth nothing—" [397]

Two births occur. One is a natural birth; the other, a spiritual birth. Natural birth takes place when we leave our premortal home to begin a new, mortal life on

---

[397] Moroni 8:22.

earth. This birth gives rise to natural beings who, in their fallen state, are enemies to God.

The gospel of Jesus Christ provides a procedure for transformation from our natural fallen state in mortality to a spiritual state in which we become alive in Christ. The gospel is a divine plan through which mortal beings are *"changed from their carnal and fallen state, to a state of righteousness, being redeemed of God, becoming his sons and daughters."* [398] In a very real and significant way, we become *"new creatures"* in Jesus Christ. [399]

This is our spiritual birth. When we die to the enticements of this world and the carnal desires of the flesh, we become new creatures through the power of the Holy Spirit. We begin a new life, a spiritual life, a life of righteousness. We become alive in Christ.

As we become alive in Christ, we seek to humble ourselves before God. We strive to become as little children. As we become alive in Christ, we seek the counsel and guidance of our loving Father and shun our worldly urges and impulses.

---

[398] Mosiah 27:25.
[399] Ibid., 27:26.

As we become alive in Christ, we *"search diligently in the light of Christ that ye may know good from evil;"* knowing that, as we *"will lay hold upon every good thing, and condemn it not, ye certainly will be a child of Christ."* [400]

Joseph Smith assures us that *"the Son of God came into the world to redeem it from the fall. But except a man be born again, he cannot see the kingdom of God. This eternal truth settles the question of all men's religion. A man may be saved, after the judgment, in the terrestrial kingdom, or in the telestial kingdom, but he can never see the celestial kingdom of God... unless he becomes as a little child, and is taught by the Spirit of God."* [401]

As we become alive in Christ, we are blessed to have the light of Christ in our lives. As Heber C. Kimball remarked:

"We are like a limb that is alive in a tree; yes, every one that are Latter-day Saints; we are united or should be as the heart of one man, and no man will be saved and gathered with Christ except they are grafted into him, for they must receive the life that flows from him in order to be exalted with him. It is upon the same

---

[400] Moroni 7:19.

[401] Smith, Joseph, *Teachings of the Prophet Joseph Smith*, p. 12.

principle that the graft that is put into a tree receives life from the tree into which it is engrafted. It is necessary that we should all be alive in Christ, and we ought to partake of his attributes and also of the attributes of his Father; then we become one with Christ as he is one with the Father. We never can enjoy the life-giving influences of the Spirit of God except we live and practice our religion, always abiding in the vine, for as the branch cannot bring forth or produce except it remain connected with the tree, so we cannot increase in light and knowledge unless we keep alive in Christ. This people are a good people and they are full of life, they are alive in Christ, and they live their religion and God blesses them." [402]

[402] Kimball, Heber C., Remarks made on April 27, 1862.

A Word About Infant Baptism

As members of the Church of Jesus Christ of Latter-day Saints, we believe and affirm that all children are innocent before God; that baptism is neither necessary nor appropriate until they reach an age of personal responsibility. The doctrine that little children are saved through the atonement of Christ is a principle established in scripture and formulated on intelligence and the justice of God.

Joseph Smith shared the following with the early members of the Church in a grove in Nauvoo:

"'Do you believe in the baptism of infants?' asks the Presbyterian. No. 'Why?' Because it is nowhere written in the Bible... Baptism is for remission of sins. Children have no sins. Jesus blessed them and said, 'Do what you have seen me do.' Children are all made alive in Christ, and those of riper years through faith and repentance." [403]

The Book of Mormon reveals the words of Christ regarding infant baptism: *"Listen to the words of Christ, your Redeemer, your Lord and your God. Behold, I came into the world not to call the righteous but*

---

[403] Smith, Joseph, *History of the Church*, 5:199.

sinners to repentance; the whole need no physician, but they that are sick; wherefore, little children are whole, for they are not capable of committing sin; wherefore the curse of Adam is taken from them in me, that it hath no power over them; and the law of circumcision is done away in me.

"And after this manner did the Holy Ghost manifest the word of God unto me; wherefore, my beloved son, I know that it is solemn mockery before God, that ye should baptize little children.

"Behold I say unto you that this thing shall ye teach—repentance and baptism unto those who are accountable and capable of committing sin; yea, teach parents that they must repent and be baptized, and humble themselves as their little children, and they shall all be saved with their little children.

"And their little children need no repentance, neither baptism. Behold, baptism is unto repentance to the fulfilling the commandments unto the remission of sins.

"But little children are alive in Christ, even from the foundation of the world; if not so, God is a partial God, and also a changeable God, and a respecter to persons; for how many little children have died without baptism. Wherefore, if little children could not be saved *without baptism, these must have gone to an endless hell.*

"Behold I say unto you, that he that supposeth that little children need baptism is in the gall of bitterness and in the bonds of iniquity, for he hath neither faith, hope, nor charity; wherefore, should he be cut off while in the thought, he must go down to hell.

"For awful is the wickedness to suppose that God saveth one child because of baptism, and the other must perish because he hath no baptism." [404]

Infants and little children are innocent and incapable of committing sin. Babies arrive in this mortal world innocent of any sin. If they were to die before they become accountable for their own actions and deeds, they justly avoid the burden of sin. It is clearly an injustice to condemn them. Little children who die before they reach the age of accountability are saved in the celestial kingdom.

Little children are redeemed by the blood of Christ and Satan has no power over them. Joseph Smith received the following vision in the Kirkland Temple: *"And I also beheld that all children who die*

---

[404] Moroni 8:8-15.

before they arrive at the years of accountability are saved in the celestial kingdom of heaven." [405]

Anyone who dies without hearing the gospel, who would have received it had they heard it, becomes an heir of the celestial kingdom. This would include *"all children who die before they arrive at the years of accountability."* [406] The prophet Joseph Smith declares that they *"are saved in the celestial kingdom of heaven."* [407]

---

[405] D&C 137:10.

[406] Smith, Joseph, *History of the Church*, 2:380, 381.

[407] Ibid.

Promise 25

The Spirit of Christ

"For behold, the Spirit of Christ is given to every man, that he may know good from evil; wherefore, I show unto you the way to judge; for every thing which inviteth to do good, and to persuade to believe in Christ, is sent forth by the power and gift of Christ; wherefore ye may know with a perfect knowledge it is of God." [408]

The Book of Mormon not only provides us with narratives relevant to the troubles of our times, but it also gives guidance, direction and counsel on how to resolve our troubles. Author, poet and essayist Eugene England writes: *"The Book of Mormon is the unique*

---

[408] Moroni 7:16.

tangible witness in the world of the most important intangible reality, the love of Christ and His power to heal and save us. I feel this power, after many readings and much study, whenever I turn to any part of the book. I immediately am brought close to tears by the Spirit of Christ that comes from every page." [409]

In the Book of Mormon, Moroni incorporated his father's teaching on the Spirit of Christ: *"For behold, the Spirit of Christ is given to every man, that he may know good from evil."* [410] The Spirit of Christ, a gift given to us by the power of Christ, is more than merely a fountain of truth; it is a vital measure of every child of our Father in heaven. [411] It is not the ideology or the expectation of a current culture or lifestyle; [412] it is, rather, an integral part of who we are. [413]

If you light a match and hold it close to a wall, then shine a flashlight on it, the matchstick will cast a shadow against the wall, but the flame will not. The flame itself is light and therefore has no shadow. John

---

[409] England, Eugene, *Converted to Christ Through the Book of Mormon,* Deseret Book, Salt Lake City, Utah.

[410] Moroni 7:16.

[411] See D&C 93:29; John 14:6, 20.

[412] See John 7:24, JST.

[413] See Romans 2:14.

described something similar when he wrote: *"This then is the message which we have heard of [Christ], and declare unto you, that God is light, and in him is no darkness at all."* [414]

Elder Penrose taught us that *"this spirit which pervades all things... is the light and life of all things, by which our heavenly Father operates, by which He is omnipotent, never had a beginning and never will have an end. It is the light of truth; it is the spirit of intelligence."* [415]

The gospel of John reveals to us that Jesus Christ is *"the true Light, which lighteth every man that cometh into the world."* [416] This is the light which *"enlighteneth your eyes, which is the same light that quickeneth your understandings."* [417] Our heavenly Father, the *"Father of lights,"* [418] endowed his beloved Son, Jesus Christ, with his own qualities, characteristics and powers [419] because Christ is

---

[414] 1 John 1:5.

[415] Penrose, Charles W., *Journal of Discourses*, 26:23.

[416] John 1:9.

[417] D&C 88:11.

[418] James 1:17.

[419] See Mosiah 15:3; D&C 93:4.

ordained to be the Light of the world. From the Doctrine and Covenants, we discover that the Spirit of Christ is the power that *"proceedeth forth from the presence of God to fill the immensity of space."* [420]

If you were to take one cubic inch of empty space in the middle of your living room, for instance, could you determine how much intelligence is in that 'empty' space? If you were to place the tip of a radio's antenna within that cubic inch of space, you could receive information and intelligence that is constantly being broadcast across the airwaves. The same would be true of television. If you could pick up a Wi-Fi signal in that cubic inch of space, you could access, by way of the internet, much of the world's known information. In a profoundly greater way, the Spirit of Christ fills the immensity of space and there is no space void of the Spirit of Christ.

"The light of Christ," wrote Bruce R. McConkie, *"is the agency of God's power and the law by which all things are governed. It is also the agency used by the Holy Ghost to manifest truth and dispense spiritual gifts to many people at one and the same time. For instance, it is as though the Holy Ghost, who is a personage of spirit, was broadcasting all truth*

---

[420] D&C 88:12.

throughout the whole universe all the time, using the light of Christ as the agency by which the message is delivered. But only those who attune their souls to the Holy Spirit receive the available revelation. It is in this way that the person of the Holy Ghost makes his influence felt in the heart of every righteous person at one and the same time." [421]

Every human born into the world benefits from this light. It is always present and will lead us to the additional light from the gift of the Holy Ghost obtained through repentance and baptism into the kingdom of God. The Spirit of Christ *"giveth light to every man that cometh into the world"* [422] with the distinct purpose that we *"may know good from evil."* [423] The Light of Christ is the human conscience, the influence found throughout the universe that gives life and light to all things. The power of discernment, our ability to distinguish good from evil comes through this Spirit of

---

[421] McConkie, Bruce R., *A New Witness for the Articles of Faith*, Deseret Book, p. 70.
[422] D&C 88:46.
[423] Moroni 7:15.

Christic. [424] It is the *"divine essence"* through which the Godhead operates upon man and in nature. [425]

The Book of Mormon also teaches us that *"the Spirit of the Lord will not always strive with man."* [426] It is a devastating tragedy when the Spirit of the Lord is withdrawn from us because of sin. The guidance and direction we need to overcome temptation is reduced, and we find it even becomes difficult to pray.

The Light of Christ is the primary blessing given to all of God's children. It is always present although it may become so dim through sin that it is almost imperceptible. It is, however, still present with everyone and can be fanned into a powerful flame that will burn bright with knowledge and understanding.

The Light of Christ is a manifestation of the glory of God. It is the instrument whereby God, a physical being, can at the same time be omnipresent. It is the light of the sun, the moon, and the stars, and the power by which all things were made. [427] It *"giveth life to all things"* and it is the *"law by which all things are*

---

[424] Ibid., vs. 12-19.

[425] Talmage, James E., *Articles of Faith*, Deseret Book, p. 488.

[426] 2 Nephi 26:11.

[427] D&C 88:7

governed." [428] It is also the power that allows God to comprehend all things. [429]

According to Parley P. Pratt, the Light of Christ *"is, in its less refined existence, the physical light that reflects from the sun, moon, and stars, and other substances, and, by reflection on the eye, makes visible the truths of the outward world. It is also in its higher degrees the intellectual light of our inward and spiritual organs, by which we reason, discern, judge, compare, comprehend, and remember the subjects within our reach. Its inspiration constitutes instinct in animal life, reason in man, and vision in the prophets, and is continually flowing from the Godhead throughout all his creations."* [430]

In other words, the same power that gives sight to our physical eyes also permits us to see with spiritual eyes. [431]

---

[428] Ibid. v. 13.

[429] Ibid. v. 41.

[430] Pratt, Parley P., *Key to the Science of Theology*, Deseret Book, p. 25.

[431] See D&C 88:6-13.

The Spirit of Christ is not the spirit essence of Jesus Christ. It is not the Holy Ghost or even the gift of the Holy Ghost. President Joseph F. Smith explained:

"The question is often asked, Is there any difference between the Spirit of the Lord and the Holy Ghost? The terms are frequently used synonymously. We often say the Spirit of God when we mean the Holy Ghost; we likewise say the Holy Ghost when we mean the Spirit of God. The Holy Ghost is a personage in the Godhead, and is not that which lighteth every man that cometh into the world. It is the Spirit of God which proceeds through Christ to the world, that enlightens every man that comes into the world, and that strives with the children of men, and will continue to strive with them, until it brings them to a knowledge of the truth and the possession of the greater light and testimony of the Holy Ghost." [432]

Bruce R. McConkie compares the gift of the Holy Ghost to the *"continuing blaze of the sun at noonday,"* and the Holy Ghost as *"a flash of lightning blazing forth in a dark and stormy night."* [433]

---

[432] Smith, Joseph F., *Gospel Doctrine,* Deseret Book, 1973. pp. 67, 68.

[433] McConkie, Bruce R., *A New Witness for the Articles of Faith,* Deseret Book, 1984. p. 262.

Our Redeemer has told us that we should *"live by every word that proceedeth forth from the mouth of God.*

"For the word of the Lord is truth, and whatsoever is truth is light, and whatsoever is light is Spirit, even the Spirit of Jesus Christ.

"And the Spirit giveth light to every man that cometh into the world; and the Spirit enlighteneth every man through the world, that hearkeneth to the voice of the Spirit.

"And every one that hearkeneth to the voice of the Spirit cometh unto God, even the Father." [434]

---

[434] D&C 84:44-47.

Promise 26

Power to Do

"And Christ hath said: If ye will have faith in me ye shall have power to do whatsoever thing is expedient in me." [435]

"He that doeth good is of God." [436]

     The comprehensive mission and purpose of the Church of Jesus Christ has always been to bring honest seekers to a knowledge of the gospel of Jesus Christ and to lead God's children to salvation and exaltation. We toil to persuade others to turn away from evil and to learn to do good. Included in the billions of earthly

---

[435] Moroni 7:33.
[436] 3 John 1:11.

inhabitants requiring salvation, we must also count ourselves.

Plato wrote that *"the first and best victory is to conquer self—to be conquered by self is, of all things, the most vile."* [437] We carry the responsibility for our own salvation and each of us has been given the power to do whatever is expedient in Christ. If we merely claim to follow Christ but lack the desire to do, we can never cultivate our faith to grow into the persuading power necessary to perfect ourselves. Then, as James says, our faith is dead. [438]

David O. McKay explained that any *"inclination to do is worth all of the good thoughts, warm feelings, and passionate prayers in which idle men indulge themselves."* [439] A purely professed belief in Christ is inadequate and will not suffice for our salvation.

The certainty of our faith in Christ is confirmed through thoughtful and obedient conduct. Speaking to the saints in 1857, Brigham Young stated:

"If Brother Brigham should take a wrong track and be shut out of the kingdom of heaven, no person

---

[437] Source Unknown.

[438] See James 2:17.

[439] Source Unknown.

will be to blame but Brother Brigham. I am the only being in heaven, earth, or hell, that can be blamed. This will equally apply to every Latter-day Saint. Salvation is an individual operation. I am the only person that can possibly save myself. When salvation is sent to me, I can reject or receive it. In receiving it, I yield implicit obedience and submission to its great Author throughout my life, and to those whom he shall appoint to instruct me; in rejecting it, I follow the dictates of my own will in preference to the will of my Creator." [440]

The counsel to *"work out your own salvation"* [441] suggests that we must do something and not simply expect God to pour out his blessings on us while we sit idlily back doing nothing. We should seek the power to do, weekly, daily, even hourly, as a confirmation of our faithful attitude and our righteous desires that through the strength and grace of God we may gain eternal life.

The Lord blesses us with the spiritual gift of faith, but that gift is activated by our power to do. We may ask God to bless the people we love and care about, (we may even ask him to bless our enemies) and he will often answer those prayers. More often than not, however, he requires we exert greater faith by

---

[440] Young, Brigham, *Conference Report*, April 1857, pp. 7, 8.
[441] See Philippians 2:12.

actually doing something to secure those needed blessings. To obtain light for his barges, the brother of Jared went right to work to molten stones. He did something and that effort of faith on his part caused a miracle to occur. [442] God acts independently but he also acts according to our faith.

In the previous promise, (Promise 25) we learned that the Spirit of Christ is in every living thing. The Spirit of the Lord is in you and has given you the power to do. I don't believe the Lord wants to do everything for us. That would be similar to Satan's plan. If we depend on someone else to do all of our work, then we have no free agency to choose.

"Evil is with us," declared Brigham Young. *"It is that influence which tempts to sin, and which has been permitted to come into the world for the express purpose of giving us an opportunity of proving ourselves before God, before Jesus Christ, our Elder Brother, before the holy angels, and before all good men, that we are determined to overcome the evil, and cleave to the good, for the Lord has given us the ability to do so. Consequently, when the evil is present with me, I have a little fighting to do, I must turn and combat it until it is eradicated from my affections, as well as*

---

[442] See Ether 3:3-5.

from my actions, that I may have power to do all the good I wish to perform. Every person is capable of this, all can bridle their tongues, and cease from every evil act from this time henceforth and forever, and do good instead." [443]

Because God loves us, he gives us a portion of his power. As we learn to use that power to do his will, he will then bless us with greater power and an increased ability to do. As Alma explains, God will grant us our desires:

"I ought not to harrow up in my desires, the firm decree of a just God, for I know that he granteth unto men according to their desire, whether it be unto death or unto life; yea, I know that he allotteth unto men according to their wills, whether they be unto salvation or unto destruction." [444]

Clearly, God awards us according to our desires. It is up to us to use that gift to do what is expedient in him. The responsibility, as Elder Talmage explained, is on us. *"Somehow the Latter-day Saints have the mistaken notion that in the end, when the day comes that the Lord will make them gods or goddesses, when*

---

[443] Young, Brigham, *Discourses of Brigham Young*, 1:91. Deseret Book, 1954.
[444] Alma 29:4.

someone lays their hands on their heads and, as it were, says to them, *You have now all that you need to be a God—go ahead*—this is not true. All that you need to be a God is in you right now. Your job is to take those crude elements within you and refine them." [445]

---
[445] Quoted by Gene R. Cook in *Living by the Power of Faith*, Deseret Book, 1985.

A Word About Keeping Your Word.

As we attempt to develop Christ-like qualities we should remember what the Savior said in the first section of the Doctrine and Covenants: *"What I the Lord have spoken, I have spoken, and I excuse not myself; and though the heavens and the earth pass away, my word shall not pass away, but shall all be fulfilled."* [446]

When the Lord says something is going to happen, then it is definitely going to happen. This is one of Christ's attributes that we should attempt to acquire if we want to be like him. If we promise to do something, we should do all that is in our power to keep and accomplish that promise.

We can control our actions to reflect our words. We can promise the Lord that we will do everything in our power to *"do whatsoever thing is expedient"* in him. [447] We don't need to do everything, but we can discipline ourselves to do some things. By doing small things we can increase our faith. As we do, we can commence to reach beyond our current capabilities.

Discipline yourself to keep your word. Don't be concerned with what you cannot accomplish. Simply

---

[446] D&C 1:38.
[447] Moroni 7:33.

exercise faith in the Lord, then do the best you can with the knowledge and power you possess. The Lord promises you: *"He that believeth on me, the works that I do shall he do also; and greater works than these shall he do."* [448]

---

[448] John 14:12.

Promise 27

The Sons and Daughters of God

"Wherefore, my beloved brethren, pray unto the Father with all the energy of heart, that ye may be filled with this love, which he hath bestowed upon all who are true followers of his Son, Jesus Christ; that ye may become the sons of God; that when he shall appear we shall be like him, for we shall see him as he is; that we may have this hope; that we may be purified even as he is pure." [449]

John the beloved recorded and affirms that *"the Word was made flesh, and dwelt among us."* The Son of God and Savior of all *"came unto his own, and his own*

---

[449] Moroni 7:48.

received him not. But as many as received him, to them gave he power to become the sons of God, even to them that believe on his name." [450]

The atonement provides the basis for birth into the kingdom of God. Jesus opened the way for the faithful and righteous to become his sons and his daughters. *"The destiny of the faithful man in this Church and the faithful woman is to become a son and daughter of God. That is the great gift that the Lord holds out to the members of the Church."* [451]

Through our faith we become sons and daughters of God. [452] When we believe and are baptized, we can begin to acquire the inherent characteristics, attributes and influences of the Holy Spirit. The more Christ-like we become, the greater those eternal qualities and characteristics will become. As the Book of Mormon teaches: *"If ye will lay hold upon every good thing, and condemn it not, ye certainly will be a child of Christ."* [453]

At the waters of Mormon, Alma taught those who had been baptized to live in love and unity without

---

[450] John 1:11, 12, 14.

[451] *Church News*, Mar. 30, 1930, p. 4.

[452] See Moroni 7:26.

[453] Moroni 7:19.

contentions, to observe the sabbath, to impart of their substance to the needy and to walk uprightly before God. The people who fled from King Noah, who believed the words of Abinadi and were baptized by Alma in the waters of Mormon attained the sacred state of becoming sons and daughters of God. The Book of Mormon records that *"thus they became the children of God."* [454]

A revelation recorded in the Doctrine and Covenants states:

"Hearken and listen to the voice of him who is from all eternity to all eternity, the Great I AM, even Jesus Christ—

"The light and the life of the world; a light which shineth in darkness and the darkness comprehendeth it not;

"The same which came in the meridian of time unto mine own, and mine own received me not;

"But to as many as received me, gave I power to become my sons; and even so will I give unto as many as will receive me, power to become my sons." [455]

---

[454] Mosiah 18:22.
[455] D&C 39:1-4.

Jesus Christ gives those who believe in his name the right and privilege to become sons and daughters of God. *"For as many as are led by the Spirit of God,"* wrote the apostle Paul, *"they are the sons of God."* [456]

What these scriptures teach us is that we can become the children of Christ right now in the present moment. We do not need to wait for some distant date in eternity. John taught us that *"now are we the sons of God and it doth not yet appear what we shall be: but we know that, when he shall appear, we shall be like him; for we shall see him as he is."* [457] Even though we are weak and wavering, we can become Christ-like right now.

The apostle John wrote of the significant blessing it is to belong to the family of Christ: *"Behold, what manner of love the Father hath bestowed upon us, that we should be called the sons of God."* [458]

Our Lord and Redeemer promises that *"we are the children of God: And if children, then heirs; heirs of*

---

[456] Romans 8:14.

[457] 1 John 3:2.

[458] 1 John 1:3.

God, and joint-heirs with Christ; if so be that we suffer with him, that we may be also glorified together." [459]

This is one of the most comforting and reassuring blessings in all Christianity. We are encouraged and uplifted by the promise and privilege to be called the children of God, restored to our rightful inheritance in his kingdom through the atonement of Christ.

If we obey the commandments and are faithful and true to the end, all that the Father has shall be given to us. What a magnificent and heartening promise! I doubt that we can fully comprehend the brilliance of this promise, but the glimmer of hope it leaves in our hearts is the confidence that if we do what the Lord requires of us, we shall become sons and daughters to God.

Every one of us is created in the image of God. When Christ returns, and we stand before him, those who have accepted and followed his teachings and gospel, will see ourselves as we see him—as a Son of God. The Savior has promised us the fulness of his kingdom and we will be entitled to the blessings of his heirs as we continue on through the eternities.

---

[459] Romans 8:17.

If we become children of God in this life, then we will achieve exaltation in the next life. The children of God here on earth who are like Christ and become one in him as he is one in the Father, become gods in the hereafter. Through the Book of Mormon, Jesus tells us that we *"shall be even as I am, and I am even as the Father; and the Father and I are one."* [460]

As we honor the gospel and obey the commandments of God, we are considered to be his children. We are heirs to his kingdom and shall receive of the fulness of his glory until we become like him. Being like the Father we become perfect. When we receive his fulness and glory and are given all that the Father has, then nothing of the Father's is withheld from us. We receive his fulness and his glory, and all things are ours, *"whether life or death, or things present, or things to come,"* [461] are all ours.

The Lord told Orson Pratt: *"My son Orson, hearken and hear and behold what I, the Lord God, shall say unto you, even Jesus Christ your Redeemer;*

---

[460] 3 Nephi 28:10.
[461] D&C 76:59.

"...Who so loved the world that he gave his own life, that as many as would believe might become the sons of God. Wherefore you are my son." [462]

The transformative power that Jesus Christ offers to believers on his name is greater than the power we might possess to improve our behavior, refine our character or lift ourselves above our base habits. It is a divine power that transforms our mortal nature to create a creature that is worthy to be deemed a son or a daughter of God.

The prophet Joseph Smith taught that all of us live in a fallen condition of corruption and carnality. We require a spiritual transformation through the influence of divine truth to allow us to become new creatures in Christ if we are to ever inherit the kingdom of God. [463] He also taught that the kingdom of our Savior is a patriarchal organization [464] presided over by Jesus Christ under the direction of the Father. When we embrace the gospel of Christ and become changed into new creatures through the power of the Holy Spirit, we are then born into the kingdom of God to become the

---

[462] D&C 34:1, 3.

[463] Quoted by Andrus, Hyrum L. in *Principles of Perfection,* Deseret Book Company, 1970.

[464] See *History of the Church*, VI, p. 252.

sons and daughters of Jesus Christ. The change of heart, or spiritual transformation, we experience is not abstract or symbolic. It is a real and literal alteration in our character. [465] Joseph Smith called those who accept the Savior's plan of life and salvation *"the begotten sons of Jesus through the gospel."* [466]

Through modern-day revelation, the Lord has promised: *"I am Jesus Christ, the Son of God, who was crucified for the sins of the world, even as many as will believe on my name, that they may become the sons of God."* [467] As sons and daughters of Christ, we become heirs of his kingdom. As heirs, we have a right to the full glory and are entitled to the greatest blessings and privileges. We become members of the family of Christ. As such, we will see his face and abide in his presence.

As the apostle John resolved: *"And every man that hath this hope in [Christ] purifieth himself, even as he is pure."* [468]

---

[465] See Mosiah 3:19; 5:7; 27:25-26.

[466] See Times and Seasons, III, September 1, 1842, pp. 904-905.

[467] D&C 35:2.

[468] 1 John 3:3.

Promise 28

All Things You Should Do

"Angels speak by the power of the Holy Ghost; wherefore, they speak the words of Christ. Wherefore, I said unto you, feast upon the words of Christ; for behold, the words of Christ will tell you all things what ye should do." [469]

In *Fiddler on the Roof*, a musical based on the book, *Tevye and his Daughters*, by Sholem Aleichem, a Jewish father of five daughters attempts to maintain his Jewish religious and cultural traditions as outside influences encroach upon his life. Tevye must cope with his strong-willed daughters, who move further

---

[469] 2 Nephi 32:3.

away from the customs of their Jewish faith and heritage, as well as with the Tsar's edict evicting the Jews from their village. Tevye explains that, amid the troubles and challenges of their careworn lives, they maintain the strength of their convictions because *"everyone knows who he is and what God wants him to do."* [470]

In the previous promise, (Promise 27) we learned that *"we are the children of God: and if children, then heirs; heirs of God, and joint-heirs with Christ."* [471] Paul testified to the people of Athens that we are all the *"offspring of God."* [472] This is who we are. But do we also understand, as Tevye claimed, to know what God wants us to do?

Life gives each of us ample and endless opportunities to exercise our free agency. When our lives are not fully aligned with the Spirit, we can often make poor and improper choices. This is not because we are bad people, but it may be a sign that we are still not *"valiant in the testimony of Jesus."* [473] Have we turned away from the world, but have not fully turned

---

[470] Aleichem, Sholem, *Tevye and his Daughters.*

[471] Romans 8: 16, 17.

[472] Acts 17:29.

[473] D&C 76:79.

to God? Is our hand on the plow but we continue to look back? Is there that *"one thing thou lackest"* yet? [474]

The Book of Mormon explains that we respond to the gospel to the extent that we believe in Christ. Faith in Christ is the preliminary principle that permits us to live the gospel. Nephi counsels that we *"must press forward with a steadfastness in Christ, having a perfect brightness of hope, and a love of God and of all men. Wherefore, if ye shall press forward, feasting upon the word of Christ, and endure to the end.... Ye shall have eternal life."* [475] Feasting on the word of Christ is equivalent to receiving direction from the Holy Ghost, which *"will tell you all things what ye should do."* [476]

Many of us like the idea of being autonomous and independent and doing things on our own. We have been blessed with good minds and with the ability to think and reason. The Lord wants us to do all that is in our power to do. Jesus even taught the Nephites that *"Ye know the things that ye must do."* [477] The danger lies in when we begin to think that we can live our lives without the Lord's help, guidance and direction. Our

---

[474] Mark 10:21.

[475] 2 Nephi 31:20.

[476] 2 Nephi 32:3.

[477] 3 Nephi 27:21.

purpose here is to grow, to become faithful and strong and to do good, but as we do, the Lord wants us to depend on him for direction.

When we have a problem, we should first attempt to work it out in our own minds. We should contemplate, deliberate and meditate on it. But we should also examine the scriptures and pray over our problems. We should seek inspiration and look for the Lord to tell us what we should do.

While teaching about the words of Christ, Nephi proposes that we *"must pray always, and not faint; that ye must not perform any thing unto the Lord save in the first place ye shall pray unto the Father in the name of Christ."* [478] Using prayer in this manner will help us receive revelation to guide us to know what we should do.

Revelation is one of the keystones of our religion. The Book of Proverbs tells us that *"Where there is no vision, the people perish."* [479] Vision is revelation. We should make use of the scriptures, the words of living prophets, and our own personal revelation to guide us in our daily decisions. Every source of the words of Christ blends together to help us

---

[478] 2 Nephi 32:9.
[479] Proverbs 29:18.

know and understand the Lord's will in telling us everything we should do.

If we desire to hear the Lord's voice, we must listen, and we must live worthily. If we are indulging in worldly activities, it will be difficult to hear the voice of the Lord. If our hearts are seeking or filled with vile thoughts, music, movies, or if we are following the promptings of Satan, it will be difficult to recognize the whisperings of the Spirit.

If, instead, we seek a life of commitment to the Savior, continually seeking and receiving his guidance and direction, we will discover that in the very process we will draw closer and closer to God. Our relationship with him will improve and intensify and we will gradually become more like him. As the Book of Mormon prophet Jacob advises: *"Continue in the way which is narrow... What can I say more?"* [480]

Studying the words of Christ will open our minds to receive revelation, even, as Alma said, *"things which never have been revealed."* [481] Not every explicit answer to our individual questions will necessarily be found in the pages of the standard works or delivered from the pulpit at General Conference. However,

---

[480] Jacob 6:11, 12.
[481] Alma 26:22.

direction to the principles that will answer those questions are there.

The Old Testament tells us that God will do nothing *"until he revealeth the secret unto his servants the prophets."* [482] But by the same token, Joseph Smith taught that *"God hath not revealed anything to Joseph, but what He will make known unto the Twelve, and even the least Saint may know all things as fast as he is able to bear them, for the day must come when no man need say to his neighbor, Know ye the Lord; for all shall know Him (who remain) from the least to the greatest. How is this to be done? It is to be done by this sealing power, and the other Comforter spoken of, which will be manifest by revelation."* [483]

The Book of Mormon is evidence to the world that *"God does inspire men in this age and generation, as well as in generations of old."* [484] It invites all of us to partake freely of the feast of the gospel of Jesus Christ. [485]

Moroni addressed those who would deny themselves of this magnificent feast: *"And again I*

---

[482] Amos 3:7 JST.

[483] Smith, Joseph, *Teachings of the Prophet Joseph Smith*, p. 149.

[484] D&C 20:11.

[485] See 2 Nephi 9:50, 51.

speak unto you who deny the revelations of God, and say that they are done away, that there are no revelations, nor prophecies, nor gifts, nor healing, nor speaking with tongues, and the interpretation of tongues; behold I say unto you, he that denieth these things knoweth not the gospel of Christ; yea, he has not read the scriptures; if so, he does not understand them." [486]

Revelation is one of the great keystones of the restoration of the gospel of Jesus Christ. The Church could not exist without it. But it also operates in the lives of those who feast upon the words of Christ that tell us all that we should do. Our task now is simply to *"see that ye do them."* [487]

---

[486] Mormon 9:7, 8.
[487] Mosiah 4:10.

Promise 29

No Power Over You

"And now, my sons, remember, remember that it is upon the rock of our Redeemer, who is Christ, the Son of God, that ye must build your foundation; that when the devil shall send forth his mighty winds, yea, his shafts in the whirlwind, yea, when all his hail and his mighty storm shall beat upon you, it shall have no power over you to drag you down to the gulf of misery and endless wo, because of the rock upon which ye are built, which is a sure foundation, a foundation whereon if men build they cannot fall." [488]

In his book, *Believing Heart: Nourishing the Seed of Faith*, Bruce Hafen writes: *"Someone once said you*

---

[488] Helaman 5:12.

can't visually tell the difference between a strand of cobweb and a strand of powerful cable—until stress is put on the strand. Our testimonies are that way, and for most of us, the days of stress for our testimonies have already begun." [489]

Our purpose on earth is to develop the attributes of God's divine nature and to be glorified in Christ. Christ came, not only to cleanse us from the stain of sin, but to renew our natures so that, over time, we can be freed from the power and appeal of transgression. A superficial testimony of the gospel will not be sufficient to withstand the full onslaught of the powers of darkness. We are fallen beings living in an immoral world and it is only through Christ that we can be transformed to a condition of spiritual strength.

We are not truly redeemed from our sins until those sins no longer have any power over us. As B. H. Roberts explains: *"After the sins of the past are forgiven, the one so pardoned will doubtless feel the force of sinful habits bearing heavily upon him.... There is an absolute necessity for some additional sanctifying grace that will strengthen poor human nature, not only to enable it to resist temptation, but also to root out*

---

[489] Hafen, Bruce C., *Believing Heart: Nourishing the Seed of Faith*, Deseret Book, 1986.

from the heart concupiscence—the blind tendency or inclination to evil. The heart must be purified, every passion, every propensity made submissive to the will, and the will of man brought into subjection to the will of God.

"Man's natural powers are unequal to this task; so, I believe, all will testify who have made the experiment. Mankind stand in some need of a strength superior to any they possess of themselves, to accomplish this work of rendering pure our fallen nature. Such strength, such power, such a sanctifying grace is conferred on man in being born of the Spirit— in receiving the Holy Ghost. Such, in the main, is its office, its work." [490]

When temptations beckon us, we must have more than a "cobweb" testimony to counter and resist the power and strength of the adversary. Our testimonies of the gospel of Christ must be built *"upon the rock of our Redeemer,... that when the devil shall send forth his mighty winds, yea, his shafts in the whirlwind, yea, when all his hail and his mighty storm shall beat upon you, It shall have no power over you,... because of the rock upon which ye are built."* [491] Our

---

[490] Roberts, B. H., *The Gospel and Man's Relationship to Deity,* Deseret Book, 1965, pp. 169-70.
[491] Helaman 5:12.

273

faith and testimony are only as secure as the foundation they are built on.

"If the stability of buildings depends largely on their foundations," writes John Stott, "so does the stability of human lives. The search for personal security is a primal instinct, but many fail to find it today. Old familiar landmarks are being obliterated. Moral absolutes which were once thought to be eternal are being abandoned." [492]

When earthly foundations crumble and falter, our hope must be secured to spiritual footings. Our firmer foundation must be unfaltering faith, true testimony and concrete conversion. These spiritual foundations will securely establish the proper meaning and perspective for the things that matter eternally.

"Foolish men build upon the shifting sands of ethics and the marshlands of human philosophies and doctrines," wrote Robert Millet. "The wise build upon the rock of revelation, heeding carefully the living oracles, lest they be 'brought under condemnation... and stumble and fall when the storms descend, and

---

[492] Stott, John, *Life in Christ,* Tyndale House. p. 22.

the winds blow, and the rains descend, and beat upon their house.'" [493]

Until we link our desires for righteousness with the edifying, revitalizing, and elevating strength of the Holy Spirit, the enticements of this world will govern the corruption of our earthly bodies. In our fallen state, we are enemies to God.

"For the natural man is an enemy to God, and has been from the fall of Adam, and will be, forever and ever, unless he yields to the enticings of the Holy Spirit, and putteth off the natural man and becometh a saint through the atonement of Christ the Lord, and becometh as a child, submissive, meek, humble, patient, full of love, willing to submit to all things which the Lord seeth fit to inflict upon him, even as a child doth submit to his father." [494]

Personal morality and ethical behavior are not enough by themselves to rescue us from our fallen state. Any human determination or physical struggle to conquer temptation and maintain an aspect of morality allowing us to return to God are profusely inadequate. We may spend our lives resisting practices that are

---

[493] Millet, Robert L., *Power of the Word: Saving Doctrines from the Book of Mormon,* Deseret Book, 1994.
[494] Mosiah 3:19.

carnal, sensual, and devilish, but we will still require a divine intervention to restore us to our spiritual selves.

Jesus Christ not only died for us, but he also came to live in us. Lasting virtue and godliness are achieved in and through Jesus Christ and in no other way. We may not fully understand how this miracle takes place, but by means of his divine power, it does. The apostle Paul noted the struggle we face with the flesh:

"I seek to subdue that sin which dwelleth in me. For I know that in me, that is, in my flesh, dwelleth no good thing; for to will is present with me, but to perform that which is good I find not, only in Christ." [495]

Once we undergo a re-creation, and sin becomes foreign to our natures, then we will experience the complete redemptive powers of the atonement of Christ. King Benjamin affirmed that *"Men drink damnation to their own souls except they humble themselves and become as little children, and believe that salvation was, and is, and is to come, in and through the atoning blood of Christ, the Lord*

---

[495] Romans 7:18, 19 JST.

Omnipotent." [496] It is inspiring to consider that Jesus Christ can and does forgive our sins.

Paul tells us to *"Be ye reconciled to God."* [497] But how can we be? We cannot overcome the world in our fallen state, but we can receive the mercy and grace of Jesus Christ and achieve a state of perfect righteousness and immortal glory. *"For he [the Father] hath made him [Christ] to be sin for us, who knew no sin; that we might be made the righteousness of God in him."* [498] We can be redeemed from sin if we allow the Savior to take our sins upon himself and impute his righteousness to us. Jesus declared to Moroni: *"My grace is sufficient for all men that humble themselves before me."* [499]

Willpower and personal resolve are both necessary to resist sin and temptation but by themselves they are insufficient. If we seek and cultivate a life in Christ, we can receive the strength to forsake and overcome the world. We demonstrate what we want in life through our choices and actions and not by what we simply profess to believe. If we want to live a Christ-centered existence, if we want to gain a

---

[496] Mosiah 3:18.
[497] 2 Corinthians 5:20.
[498] Ibid., 21.
[499] Ether 12:27.

stronger testimony of the gospel, if we want to develop the gift of faith or charity, if we want to obtain eternal life—we can! All of this can be ours if we desire it more than we desire the things of the world.

The greatest challenge we face is to build our lives on a sure foundation. There is safety only in Christ. As we attempt to purify our desires and to live worthy lives, we place ourselves in a position to build a house of faith where Christ and his Spirit can dwell. In his word and through his infinite power we can obtain a deeply rooted testimony of the gospel.

Nephi voiced our need to rely wholly upon Christ: *"I know in whom I have trusted. My God hath been my support."* [500]

---

[500] 2 Nephi 4:19, 20.

Promise 30

The Gift...of the Holy Ghost

"And blessed are they who shall seek to bring forth my Zion at that day, for they shall have the gift and the power of the Holy Ghost; and if they endure unto the end they shall be lifted up at the last day, and shall be saved in the everlasting kingdom of the Lamb; and whoso shall publish peace, yea, tidings of great joy, how beautiful upon the mountains shall they be." [501]

President Martin Van Buren asked Joseph Smith how The Church of Jesus Christ of Latter-day Saints differed

---

[501] 1 Nephi 13:37.

from the other religions of the day. The prophet told him that we differed in mode of baptism, and the gift of the Holy Ghost by the laying on of hands. [502]

The Holy Ghost is a personage of Spirit and is one in purpose with God the Father and his Son. The Holy Ghost performs a distinct and unique mission in the lives of God's children. The gift of the Holy Ghost, on the other hand, is the right to receive divine direction, heavenly manifestations, and spiritual gifts. It is an essential ordinance of Christ's gospel and a definite criterion for salvation.

The gift of the Holy Ghost is one of the first four principles and ordinances of the gospel, [503] intrinsically connected to faith in the Lord Jesus Christ, repentance, and baptism by immersion for the remission of sins. Together they constitute the only way in which we can be cleansed of our sins, become untainted from the world and be found worthy to return to our Father in heaven.

After the re-birth of baptism, the gift of the Holy Spirit inducts us into the kingdom of God and creates in us a new person. Without the gift of the Holy Ghost we do not rightfully belong to the true Church of Jesus

---

[502] See *History of the Church* 4:42.
[503] Articles of Faith:4.

Christ. The gifts, attendance and manifestations of the Holy Ghost are indications of spiritual living and approval.

Inspiration from the Spirit of the Lord is available to all of humanity at anytime and anywhere provided we are in tune with the Spirit. The gift of the Holy Ghost differs in that it is a constant and abiding companion to those who receive it. This gift is evident as we demonstrate faith in Christ, repent of our sins, are baptized, and seek earnestly to follow the Savior.

One of the greatest blessings accompanying the gift of the Holy Ghost is sanctification. It is through the gift of the Holy Ghost that we are cleansed of sin and become born of God. We become a new creature when we are sanctified by the Holy Ghost. Our previous behaviors, practices, passions and personality are transformed. We come to witness *"a mighty change in us, or in our hearts, that we have no more disposition to do evil, but to do good continually."* [504] We feel differently about ourselves and we feel differently about the people around us. The yearnings and enticements of the world are removed from our hearts, and we become more like the Savior in our attitudes

---

[504] Mosiah 5:2.

and behaviors. These changes are part of the purifying powers of the Holy Ghost.

Spiritual purification or being *"sanctified by the reception of the Holy Ghost"* [505] through baptism by fire sears the sin, sensuality, wickedness and immorality from our penitent hearts like a fire. Cleansed of all iniquity we literally become new creatures of the Holy Ghost. This constitutes the process of being born again.

Bruce R. McConkie taught that it is the Holy Spirit *"that erases carnality and brings us into a state of righteousness. We become clean when we actually receive the fellowship and companionship of the Holy Ghost. It is then that sin and dross and evil are burned out of our souls as though by fire. The baptism of the Holy Ghost is the baptism of fire."* [506]

Through sanctification we can, over time, become pure and spotless. The culminating effect of repentance and baptism, through the Holy Ghost and baptism by fire, cleanses our hearts and desires and our spirits are made pure. Paul wrote: *"If any man be in*

---

[505] 3 Nephi 27:20.
[506] McConkie, Bruce R., *A New Witness for the Articles of Faith*, Deseret Book Company, 1985 p. 290.

Christ, he is a new creature: old things are passed away; behold, all things are become new." [507]

The gift of the Holy Ghost is among the greatest blessings offered to members of Christ's church. The gift of the Holy Ghost is the key to all other spiritual gifts within the church. This includes the gifts of healing and being healed, prophecy and revelation, speaking in tongues and the interpretation of tongues. These numerous, diverse gifts are available to us in accordance with our faith and diligence in seeking them. We have access to them the same as any of God's children throughout history. However, these distinct gifts are manifest only when we have received the gift of the Holy Ghost by the laying on of hands. Worthiness and the necessity of divine intervention or assistance make us eligible to receive these gifts of the Holy Ghost.

The varied and diverse gifts from the Holy Ghost are needed throughout our lives in every situation or circumstance. They have been indispensable during every era and age. They are no less a necessity in the turbulent times of this final dispensation. But these gifts must be cultivated. Receiving the ordinance by itself is insufficient to keep the Holy Ghost operating in

---

[507] 2 Corinthians 5:17.

our lives. As we are trying to live by gospel principles, demonstrating love toward God and toward his other children, remembering to be humble and kind, then we will witness the Holy Ghost operating in our lives. We should prepare our hearts to receive the Holy Ghost and we should live worthily to retain it. Unless we do this, the Holy Ghost will not function in our lives.

"A man may receive the Holy Ghost, and it may descend upon him and not tarry with him." [508]

The Holy Ghost enables us to bear witness of Jesus Christ and of all divine truth. It provides direction, guidance and warning when needed. It also enables us to distinguish and discern between right and wrong.

"The Holy Ghost," taught Parley P. Pratt, *"quickens all the intellectual faculties, increases, enlarges, expands, and purifies all the natural passions and affections, and adapts them, by the gift of wisdom, to their lawful use. It inspires, develops, cultivates and matures all the fine-toned sympathies, joys, tastes, kindred feelings, and affections of our nature."* [509] It is through the Holy Ghost that we come to the knowledge of God. It touches our hearts as we hear and read inspired words. The scriptures are more

---

[508] D&C 130:23.

[509] Pratt, Parley P., *Key to the Science of Theology*, p. 61.

clearly understood through its power. The heavens open to us and ignorance and darkness dissipate.

The loftiest blessing offered to us through the Holy Ghost lies in the spiritual refinement that takes place within our hearts. Baptism by water cleanses us. Baptism by fire removes our past imperfections until nothing impure remains. This cleansing is referred to in the Book of Mormon as the *"refiner's fire."* [510] Metals are often purified using intense heat. The impurities, known as dross, are burned away and the metal becomes tougher and stronger. If we want to be worthy to return to our Father's presence, we need the purifying and sanctifying process of a spiritual refiner's fire.

The resurrected Savior instructed the Nephites to *"repent... and come unto me and be baptized in my name, that ye may be sanctified by the reception of the Holy Ghost, that ye may stand spotless before me at the last day."* [511]

As we submit to the promptings of the Holy Ghost, it will guide us toward an improved awareness and realization of a Christ-like persona. The apostle Paul affirms in his epistle to the Galatians that *"the fruit*

---

[510] 3 Nephi 24:2.
[511] 3 Nephi 27:20.

of the Spirit is love, joy, peace, longsuffering, gentleness, goodness, faith,

"Meekness, temperance; against such there is no law.

"And they that are Christ's have crucified the flesh with the affections and lusts.

"If we live in the Spirit, let us also walk in the Spirit." [512]

When we live worthy of the companionship of the Holy Ghost, it will bless us with increased virtue, vision and power.

Although the gift of the Holy Ghost is given to us only once following baptism, its blessings and benefits are continuous throughout our lives. The Holy Ghost can be a *"constant companion,"* [513] guiding, directing and sustaining us as we live worthy of such blessings. The gift of the Holy Ghost is designed to assist us in attaining our divine potential.

Modern revelation states: *"I will tell you in your mind and in your heart, by the Holy Ghost, which shall*

---

[512] Galatians 5:22-25.
[513] D&C 121:46.

come upon you and which shall dwell in your heart. *Now, behold this is the spirit of revelation."* [514] By following the promptings of the Holy Ghost, we will continue to progress and grow spiritually and experience greater gifts. Its constant companionship will seal the ordinances given to us. Receiving the gift of the Holy Ghost does not, in and of itself, guarantee us of any particular blessing or gift. All the gifts of the Spirit are conditional. Faith, humility and personal worthiness are the requisite characteristics for obtaining the gifts and companionship of the Holy Ghost.

Paul counsels us to *"stir up the gift of God, which is in thee."* [515] Not every gift will be granted to every individual but by utilizing the gifts we are given to bless and enlighten others, we can be filled with charity and gain eternal life.

The Holy Ghost will speak comfort to our souls. It stirs our spiritual senses. It fills our lives with perfect love and hope. It reveals eternal truths and the splendors of heaven. It lifts our spirits and brings peace to our hearts. It directs our souls toward everlasting life. Our greatest ambition in this life should be to procure

---

[514] D&C 8:2, 3.
[515] 2 Timothy 1:6.

the promise of the constant companionship and sanctifying power of the Holy Ghost.

Moroni closes the Book of Mormon with his frequently quoted invitation to examine the truthfulness of its glorious message by asking God and obtaining a sure witness from the Holy Ghost:

"Behold, I would exhort you that when ye shall read these things, if it be wisdom in God that ye should read them, that ye would remember how merciful the Lord hath been unto the children of men, from the creation of Adam even down until the time that ye shall receive these things, and ponder it in your hearts.

"And when ye shall receive these things, I would exhort you that ye would ask God, the Eternal Father, in the name of Christ, if these things are not true; and if ye shall ask with a sincere heart, with real intent, having faith in Christ, he will manifest the truth of it unto you, by the power of the Holy Ghost.

"And by the power of the Holy Ghost ye may know the truth of all things." [516]

The cherished companionship of the Holy Ghost will enlighten us on our mortal journey so that we are

---

[516] Moroni 10:3-5.

able to return to the presence of our celestial Father and receive the most treasured gift of all—the gift of life eternal.

Promise 31

The Truth of All Things

"And by the power of the Holy Ghost ye may know the truth of all things." [517]

In the previous promise, (Promise 30) we learned that the Holy Ghost is a revelator, bearing record of Jesus Christ and of all truth. It imparts gospel truths to the righteous who are seeking to become like the Savior. *"The best way to obtain truth and wisdom,"* according to the prophet Joseph Smith, *"is not to ask it from*

---

[517] Moroni 10:5.

books, but to go to God in prayer, and obtain divine teaching." [518]

From our earliest childhood days, we are taught how to learn through study. We are taught by parents and teachers the cognitive, logical process of fine tuning our mental capacities. We are trained to concentrate on the material and to discover the subject at hand. But spiritual matters founded in faith are learned and understood through revelation. When we learn through revelation, we attain understanding and insight made known directly to our hearts and minds through the Holy Ghost.

You may recall that Nephi's brothers could not grasp what their father had taught them, *"For he truly spake many great things unto them, which were hard to be understood, save a man should inquire of the Lord."* When they told Nephi, *"We cannot understand the words which our father hath spoken,"* Nephi asked, *"Have ye inquired of the Lord?"* Of course, they hadn't, making the excuse that *"the Lord maketh no such thing known unto us."* Nephi responded by presenting them with the same formula that Moroni shares with us at the end of the Book of Mormon. He informed them that

---

[518] Smith, Joseph F., *Teachings of the Prophet Joseph Smith*, Deseret Book, p. 191.

"If ye will not harden your hearts, and ask... in faith, believing that ye shall receive, with diligence in keeping [the] commandments, surely these things shall be made known unto you." [519]

The Savior's approach to learning is spoken of in John: *"If any man will do his will, he shall know of the doctrine."* [520] We learn by faith when we do what the Lord commands, seeking at the same time for the sanctioning approval of the Holy Ghost.

Learning by faith requires hope in what is unseen but true. [521] We experience the blessings of an honest tithe only after we make that offering. We attain the benefits of a healthier lifestyle as we observe the Word of Wisdom. We gain a witness of the truthfulness of the Book of Mormon when we follow Moroni's directive to read, ponder and pray. As we practice the principles and precepts of the gospel, we grow in faith until we actually know with certainty. Some truths will only be understood by the faithful.

Paul expounds on the educative effect of the Holy Ghost: *"My speech and my preaching was not with*

---

[519] See 1 Nephi 15:3-11.
[520] John 7:17.
[521] See Alma 32:21.

enticing words of man's wisdom, but in demonstration of the Spirit and of power:

"That your faith should not stand in the wisdom of men, but in the power of God...

"As it is written, Eye hath not seen, nor ear heard, neither have entered into the heart of man, the things which God hath prepared for them that love him.

"But God hath revealed them unto us by his Spirit: for the Spirit searcheth all things, yea, the deep things of God. For what man knoweth the things of a man, save the spirit of man which is in him? even so the things of God knoweth no man, but the Spirit of God.

"Now we have received, not the spirit of the world, but the spirit which is of God; that we might know the things that are freely given to us of God. Which things also we speak, not in the words which man's wisdom teacheth, but which the Holy Ghost teacheth; comparing spiritual things with spiritual.

"But the natural man receiveth not the things of the Spirit of God: for they are foolishness unto him: neither can he know them, because they are spiritually discerned. But he that is spiritual judgeth all things, yet he himself is judged of no man. For who hath known *the mind of the Lord, that he may instruct him? But we have the mind of Christ."* [522]

The promise made in the Book of Mormon focuses on the knowledge of things pertaining to the kingdom of God. James advises those who seek wisdom to *"ask of God, that giveth to all men liberally, and upbraideth not; and it shall be given him."* [523] The knowledge revealed through the Holy Ghost encompasses the marvels of eternity, the revelations of the restoration and the visions of past and future events. It is wisdom beyond the prudence and knowledge of the wisest human intellects.

When we righteously serve God, we become heirs to the riches of his kingdom. These riches include wisdom and knowledge of the greatest celestial truths. A quote from Marion G. Romney states: *"Such truth is not to be had through man's ordinary learning processes. His sensory powers are calculated and adapted to deal only with the things of this telestial earth. Without revelation, man's intellect is wholly*

---

[522] 1 Corinthians 2:4, 5, 9-16.
[523] James 1:5.

inadequate for the discovery of the ultimate truth with which the gospel deals." [524]

The greatest understanding is knowledge obtained through revelation. The *"glory of God is intelligence"* [525] and God promises all the wisdom of heaven to the faithful. In the Sermon on the Mount, Christ tells his disciples to *"Ask, and it shall be given you; seek, and ye shall find; knock, and it shall be opened unto you: for every one that asketh receiveth; and he that seeketh findeth; and to him that knocketh it shall be opened."* [526]

All of the doctrines of the Church of Jesus Christ are rooted in revelation. Certain truths are grasped and understood only by righteousness. Some truths are revealed and recognized only by faithfulness. *"Purity, not intellect,"* observed Joseph F. McConkie, *"is the prime requisite for the knowledge of God. Knowledge that can be obtained independent of purity and righteousness is without the power of salvation. Only that knowledge that comes from God through the medium of the Holy Spirit has the power to sanctify the soul and prepare one to stand in the divine presence.*

---

[524] Romney, Marion G., *Look to God and Live,* Deseret Book, p. 65.
[525] D&C 93:36.
[526] Matthew 7:7, 8.

Such is the 'Spirit of truth', a spirit which the 'world cannot receive.'" [527] [528]

We cannot rightfully follow the Savior in ignorance. Those who seek the light of heaven will find the companionship of the Holy Ghost and the spirit of revelation will bring them insight and understanding. As demonstrated by Nephi's brothers earlier in this promise, there are certain truths that the unrighteous and unfaithful will never comprehend.

All true doctrine deals in spiritual matters and is revealed and confirmed through the power of the Holy Ghost. Bruce R. McConkie offers this insight: *"We do not come to a knowledge of God and his laws through intellectuality, or by research, or by reason. They are important enough in their sphere, but when contrasted with spiritual endowments, they are of but slight and passing worth. From an eternal perspective, what each of us needs is a Ph.D. in faith and righteousness. The things that will profit us everlastingly are not the power to reason, but the ability to receive revelation; not the truths learned by study, but the knowledge gained by*

---

[527] John 14:17.

[528] McConkie, Joseph F., *The Spirit of Truth*, (from To Be Learned is Good if...) Bookcraft, p. 231.

faith; not what we know about the things of the world, but our knowledge of God and his laws." [529]

To progress eternally we need a knowledge of truth which is grounded by an assurance borne of the Spirit. It is important to learn math, science, history, language and art, but certain knowledge is more vital and significant in an eternal perspective. Knowing the laws of science can be useful. Knowing the existence of an infinite and eternal God is vital. Understanding algebra and geometry can be helpful. Knowing that Jesus is the Christ and that salvation comes through him is essential. Knowing programming and coding can be valuable. Knowing that the Book of Mormon is the word of God and that Joseph Smith is a prophet of God who restored lost knowledge and authority is crucial.

Some truths simply matter more than others. Earthly truths are relative and can change. Eternal truths are constant and consistent. Social truths shift with changing world views. Eternal truths are absolute and are not determined by a consensus from the masses. The Holy Ghost differentiates these truths for us.

---

[529] McConkie, Bruce R., *Conference Report*, Apr. 1971, pp. 99.

Neal Maxwell instructed that: *"Facts are useful, everlasting truths are critical. So much of real education consists of acquiring perspective about everlasting truths so that we can then manage, successfully, the transitory factual things, for tactical choices do crowd in upon us hour by hour. Knowing the facts about a bus schedule, for instance, is helpful, but such facts are clearly not the emancipating truths Jesus spoke of as being necessary to experience real freedom."* [530]

Revelation is personal. A truth revealed to a parent or spouse or church leader will not save someone else. The truth of the doctrines must be learned and confirmed to each of us, individually, by the Holy Ghost. The strength of our testimonies depends on our personal witness being grounded in essential, eternal truth verified through the Holy Ghost. We are commanded to *"Receive the Holy Ghost."* We cannot receive the Holy Ghost, according to Joseph Smith, without receiving revelations. [531]

The development of our testimonies may be simple at first and centered mainly on feelings rather

---

[530] Maxwell, Neal A., baccalaureate address delivered at Ricks College, 25 Apr. 1978.

[531] See Smith, Joseph F., *Teachings of the Prophet Joseph Smith,* Deseret Book, p. 328.

than knowledge. But we are expected to search the scriptures, to study and grow in understanding. Receiving the gift of the Holy Ghost means that we also receive the responsibility to rely on it and draw on it. The Doctrine and Covenants explains that we should *"grow up in"* the Father, *"and receive a fulness of the Holy Ghost."* [532] As we learn line-upon-line, growing in the witness of truth, our testimonies will become resolute and unwavering. *"The Spirit manifesteth truth; and whoso is enlightened by the Spirit shall obtain benefit therefrom."* [533] Our convictions of spiritual truth will begin to solidify.

Joseph Smith observed: *"We consider that God has created man with a mind capable of instruction, and a faculty which may be enlarged in proportion to the heed and diligence given to the light communicated from heaven to the intellect; and that the nearer man approaches perfection, the clearer are his views, and the greater his enjoyments, till he has overcome the evils of his life and lost every desire for sin; and like the ancients, arrives at that point of faith*

---

[532] D&C 109:15.
[533] D&C 91:4, 5.

where he is wrapped in the power and glory of his Maker and is caught up to dwell with Him." [534]

The promise of knowing the truth of all things is given to all faithful seekers. It is not based on position but on personal worthiness. It is not offered according to office but according to the purity of our hearts.

---

[534] Smith, Joseph F., *Teachings of the Prophet Joseph Smith*, Deseret Book Co., p. 51.

Chapter Three

The Voice of the Lord

Aaron, a son of King Mosiah, presented a question to the unbelieving Amalekites. He asked: *"Believest thou that the Son of God shall come to redeem mankind from their sins?"* He followed this question with a powerful witness of the Savior, testifying that: *"There could be no redemption for mankind save it were through the death and sufferings of Christ, and the atonement of his blood."* [535] The Book of Mormon was written *"by the spirit of prophecy and of revelation,"* to convince *"the Jew and Gentile that Jesus is the Christ, the Eternal God."* [536]

---

[535] Alma 21:7, 9.
[536] Title Page, *The Book of Mormon*.

The great promise and testimony of the Book of Mormon is that: *"The gate of heaven is open unto all, even to those who will believe on the name of Jesus Christ, who is the Son of God."* [537] In plain and simple language that leaves no room for confusion or misinterpretation, the Book of Mormon testifies again and again of Jesus Christ through whom salvation comes.

A revelation in the Doctrine and Covenants instructs us that the Book of Mormon is the voice of the Lord:

"These words are not of men nor of man, but of me; wherefore, you shall testify they are of me and not of man;

"For it is my voice which speaketh them unto you; for they are given by my Spirit unto you, and by my power you can read them one to another; and save it were by my power you could not have them;

"Wherefore, you can testify that you have heard my voice, and know my words." [538]

---

[537] Helaman 3:28.
[538] D&C 18:34-36.

Everyone who reads the Book of Mormon with a pure heart and with a desire to know of its truthfulness, can hear the sweet whisperings of the Holy Spirit. The Lord promises us a *"more sure witness"* of the truth of these things borne of the Holy Ghost. *"It is the Spirit that beareth witness, because the Spirit is truth."* [539]

The most effective way to discover truth in the spiritual realm is to ask God. *"Ask, and it shall be given you,"* [540] Jesus tells us. To which James adds, *"Let him ask in faith, nothing wavering."* [541]

The precise procedure for obtaining pure knowledge of spiritual truth, including the truth of the Book of Mormon, was given to us by Moroni:

"Behold, I would exhort you that when ye shall read these things, if it be wisdom in God that ye should read them, that ye would remember how merciful the Lord hath been unto the children of men, from the creation of Adam even down until the time that ye shall receive these things, and ponder it in your hearts.

---

[539] 1 John 5:6.
[540] Matthew 7:7.
[541] James 1:6.

"And when ye shall receive these things, I would exhort you that ye would ask God, the Eternal Father, in the name of Christ, if these things are not true; and if ye shall ask with a sincere heart, with a real intent, having faith in Christ, he will manifest the truth of it unto you, by the power of the Holy Ghost.

"And by the power of the Holy Ghost ye may know the truth of all things." [542]

The pages of the Book of Mormon are saturated with a language, a lucidity, and a logic that emerge unmistakably into the hearts and minds of everyone who seriously searches the truth of its message. The Holy Spirit is the interpretive key that opens the knowledge of its precepts and principles.

One purpose for our earthly existence is to learn to walk by faith. We must learn to develop our powers of faith in Christ in this life. As we do, God will not allow our faith to go unanswered. We are promised that evidence and witnesses will *"follow them that believe."* [543]

---

[542] Moroni 10:3-5.
[543] Mark 16:17.

God is not against giving signs. He is willing to provide evidence and prove all his works. However, evidence will only follow faith, it will never precede it. Signs may be offered to assist with the development of an already present faith, they are not offered in place of faith. The significance of signs, evidence, and proof is lost on anyone who has not already developed a degree of faith.

In proving the truthfulness of the promises found in the Book of Mormon, we should seek faith before seeking signs. Moroni stated, *"I... would show unto the world that faith is things which are hoped for and not seen; wherefore, dispute not because ye see not, for ye receive no witness until after the trial of your faith."* [544]

The Book of Mormon, in addition to other scripture, allows us to hear the voice of the Spirit. The Lord is speaking to us, giving us revelation and instruction, through its passages and verses. The Book of Mormon was not only given by the voice of the Lord through revelation, it also allows us to hear his voice as we delve into its pages. It renews in our hearts a

---

[544] Ether 12:6.

profound feeling of peace and love manifest through the Spirit.

The Book of Mormon is a witness for the divinity of Jesus Christ. It is also a witness of the truthfulness of the Bible. Its specific purpose is to reveal the great things that the Lord has done for us. It brings us to a knowledge of a Savior through the testimony of the early inhabitants of the Americas. It has restored plain and precious truths of the gospel of Jesus Christ that had been lost to the world. The Book of Mormon will prepare the faithful for the second coming of Jesus Christ and his millennial reign.

The Holy Bible is one witness to the divinity of Jesus Christ. The Book of Mormon is another witness of the Savior. The Book of Mormon testifies that "*I shall speak unto the Jews and they shall write it; and I shall also speak unto the Nephites and they shall write it; ...*

"*And it shall come to pass that the Jews shall have the words of the Nephites, and the Nephites shall have the words of the Jews; and the Nephites and the Jews shall have the words of the lost tribes of Israel; and the lost tribes of Israel shall have the words of the Nephites and the Jews...*

"And my word... shall be gathered in one." [545]

Brigham Young also testified: *"No man can say that this book (laying his hand on the Bible) is true... and at the same time say, that the Book of Mormon is untrue... There is not that person on the face of the earth who has had the privilege of learning the Gospel of Jesus Christ from these two books, that can say that one is true, and the other is false. No Latter-day Saint, no man or woman, can say the Book of Mormon is true, and at the same time say that the Bible is untrue. If one be true, both are."* [546]

More than any other book, the Book of Mormon is Christ centered. It leads us to know the Lord and it motivates us to do good. God is its author. It was written by prophets who knew the Savior and had personally partaken of his goodness and grace. It was prepared by seers who saw in vision the obstacles, challenges and personal difficulties our generation would face, [547] making the Book of Mormon eternally applicable and relatable. Its message is meaningful, reliable and

---

[545] 2 Nephi 29:12-14.

[546] Young, Brigham, *Journal of Discourses*, 1:38.

[547] See Mormon 8:35; 9:30.

comforting. It was written specifically for us and therefore speaks directly to us.

I have a tremendous love for the Book of Mormon. I sense a spirit of peace and righteousness settle over me whenever I read from it. I feel the Savior's love flow from its pages. The Spirit of the Lord has borne witness to me that the Book of Mormon is true. The prophet Joseph Smith was the seer raised up to translate the ancient record and sacred scripture with its divine and inspiring message.

About the Author

Bill Wylson is the author of over 45 publications dealing with family values, religious issues and religious education. His work has appeared in *The Ensign, This People, Liberty Magazine, Success,* and others. Bill graduated from the Columbia School of Broadcasting in Hollywood, CA as a commercial copywriter. He wrote trade journal ads for a major advertising agency in Los Angeles and public service announcements for a Los Angeles television station. He also wrote and produced corporate video presentations.

Bill has written and edited policy and procedure manuals, company newsletters, brochures, employee handbooks, job descriptions, resumes, press releases, and public service announcements. He has also worked as a grant writer for various non-profit agencies, developing and implementing million-dollar programs supported by local, state and federal funds.

He has served as a volunteer Board Member of Advocates of Single Parent Youth, Special Fun Games for the Disabled, and on the Boards of Arts and Theater Councils. He has also served on Advisory Committees for the Volunteer Center of Los Angeles and on the United Way Government Affairs Committee.

Bill served a full-time mission in Cordoba, Argentina. He has also taught Seminary classes, Gospel Doctrine classes, Elders' Quorums and High Priest Groups. Bill has served in three Elders' Quorum presidencies, one High Priests' Group and two bishoprics.

Bill Wylson currently lives with his wife in Salt Lake City, Utah.

Other Books by Bill Wylson

Hieroglyphs, Golden Plates and Typos: How 'Corrections' in the Book of Mormon Prove Its Authenticity.

"Hieroglyphs, Golden Plates and Typos has a single, narrowly defined purpose: to draw attention to 'corrections' in the Book of Mormon as evidences that the book is precisely what it claims to be: an ancient text originally inscribed upon metal plates over the course of centuries by a number of historians."

"Hieroglyphs, Golden Plates and Typos presents excellent evidence of the claims that the Book of Mormon is an ancient writing inscribed on metal plates which was later translated by the Prophet Joseph Smith. Wylson convincingly demonstrates how the original authors of the Book of Mormon corrected any 'typos' or 'slips of the stylus,' as he calls them, and presents them as evidence of the origin of the Book of Mormon. A very interesting and faith-building book."

Seven Success Strategies for Latter-day Saints

"Seven Success Strategies is an outstanding book by LDS author Bill Wylson. This is a book about living a successful life based on basic gospel principles. Each strategy is presented is separate chapters with a 3-step challenge at the end of each chapter. It is filled with actionable insights to realizing true success in all aspects of life."

"This book came at a great time in my life, I found motivation through it and the principles of the seven strategies for success are very well outlined. They are simple truths that we easily lose sight of as we get busy in life. Bill Wylson does a great job of explaining the way to success through great gospel truths. I have a new-found motivation with a clear path and new perspective."

Three Minutes Eighteen Seconds.

Bill Wylson "asks us to imagine President Monson's last conference address as a three-minute interview with the prophet. This context adds additional immediacy to President Monson's message."

"This is a wonderful short sweet book with all kinds a great information for everyone. I'm glad I purchased this, and I will re-read it over and over. I recommend this book to everyone."

Also available in Spanish.

www.ingramcontent.com/pod-product-compliance
Lightning Source LLC
LaVergne TN
LVHW051727080426
835511LV00018B/2917